Twayne's United States Authors Series

Sylvia E. Bowman, *Editor*
INDIANA UNIVERSITY

Ernest Hemingway

ERNEST HEMINGWAY

by EARL ROVIT

University of Louisville

TWAYNE PUBLISHERS

A DIVISION OF G. K. HALL & CO., BOSTON

FOR HONEY

"And this too remember; a serious writer is not to be confounded with a solemn writer. A serious writer may be a hawk or a buzzard, or even a popinjay, but a solemn writer is always a bloody owl."

—*Death in the Afternoon*

Contents

About the Author

Earl Rovit, a member of the English Department of the University of Louisville, is the author of *Herald to Chaos* (1960), a study of the novels of Elizabeth Madox Roberts. He has contributed articles on American literature, American studies, and modern European fiction to various journals and periodicals. He was Fulbright Professor of American Literature at the University of Freiburg in 1960-61.

Preface

MY ORIGINAL INTENTIONS for the structure of *Ernest Hemingway* were to dispose of Hemingway the man in the opening chapter and to survey his work chronologically in the succeeding chapters. Two things happened to make this sensible plan impossible. After I had disposed of Hemingway in Chapter I, he wouldn't stay out of the succeeding chapters. At first I fought against him, but ultimately I capitulated. My plans to treat his work in successive chronological fashion likewise met with disaster. The whole body of Hemingway's writing proved to be of such a single piece that individual fictions written twenty years apart demanded to be treated together. Again I fought, and again I surrendered unconditionally. If it were possible to blame something besides my own cowardly irresolution, I would claim that Hemingway and his books determined the composition of my book. It is not likely that such a claim would be honored.

In general the structure of this study proceeds along the following lines. Chapter I introduces Hemingway and makes an initial attempt to place him in the context of his times and to follow the course of his life. Chapter II, which deals with the formation of his prose aesthetic, investigates such matters as his aesthetic concern with emotion, the major influences on his characteristic techniques up to the time of his earliest publications, a preliminary investigation of his style, and a discussion of his attitude toward his audience. Chapter III is an extended investigation of his typical characters—heroes and heroines—and an attempt to see how these fit into his aesthetic. Chapter IV studies the characteristic structures of his fiction and tries to relate these structures to the overriding aesthetic. In Chapter V the famous Hemingway "code" is analyzed extensively, and there is an attempt to fit this code into the cumulative context of the aesthetic which has been developing from Chapter II. Chapter VI deals almost exclusively with Hemingway's metaphysic of time and its relation to the code and the aesthetic; there is also a further examination of Hemingway's style in this chapter which attempts to relate the style to the aesthetic in a more complex manner than did the earlier investigation. Chapter VII, an essay in literary exegesis on *The Sun Also Rises*, is hopefully designed to be an illustrative exemplar of the critical hypotheses drawn from the first six chapters. And Chapter VIII attempts to sum up the results of the introductory survey and to indicate the shape of Hemingway's achievements, as well as his significance in literary history.

Inserted within the general discussion are fairly detailed explications of many of Hemingway's fictions; these include "Big Two-Hearted River," "In Another Country," "The Undefeated," "A Clean Well-Lighted Place," "Fifty Grand," "The Snows of Kilimanjaro," "The Short Happy Life of Francis Macomber," *A Farewell to Arms*, *For Whom the Bell Tolls*, and *The Old Man and the Sea*. Unlike the discussion of *The Sun Also Rises*, the exegeses of the other fictions are usually subordinate to the illustration or examination of some specific point in the discussion. I have been more interested in investigating the total contour of Hemingway's fiction than in providing a series of readings of his individual fictions. The reader is referred to the index for citations of specific stories.

I should like to acknowledge the generosity of the University of Louisville Research Fund Committee which accorded me a grant through which I was able to secure the necessary time to prepare this study.

EARL ROVIT

August, 1962
Louisville, Kentucky

Acknowledgments

Quotations from the following works of Ernest Hemingway are used by permission of Charles Scribner's Sons: *A Farewell to Arms, Across the River and into the Trees, Death in the Afternoon, For Whom the Bell Tolls, Green Hills of Africa, The Old Man and the Sea, Winner Take Nothing, In Our Time;* "Big-Two-Hearted River," "In Another Country," "The Snows of Kilimanjaro," "The Undefeated," "The Three-Day Blow," "A Clean Well-Lighted Place." Copyright 1925, 1926, 1929, 1932, 1933, 1936, 1940, 1952 Charles Scribner's Sons; renewal copyright 1953, 1954, 1957, 1960, 1961 Ernest Hemingway. Copyright 1933, 1935 Charles Scribner's Sons; renewal copyright 1961, 1963 Mary Hemingway.

For permission to quote from the following works, I am indebted to these writers and publishers: D. S. Savage, *The Withered Branch,* Eyre & Spottiswoode; George Plimpton, "Ernest Hemingway," *The Paris Review;* Oscar Cargill, *Intellectual America,* The Macmillan Company; Lillian Ross, "Portrait of Hemingway," *The New Yorker;* Jean-Paul Sartre, "American Novelists in French Eyes," *The Atlantic Monthly;* T. S. Eliot, "The Hollow Men," Harcourt Brace & World, Inc.

And finally I should like to acknowledge two other cases of indebtedness: to Sylvia E. Bowman for intelligent and conscientious editorial supervision; and to Richard G. McLaughlin who first taught me to listen to the silences in Hemingway's prose.

Chronology

1899   Ernest Hemingway born (July 21) in Oak Park, Illinois, son of Dr. Clarence E. and Grace Hall Hemingway.

1917   After graduation from Oak Park High School, works as a reporter on the Kansas City *Star*.

1918   Enlists as an ambulance driver for the Red Cross in Italy; is severely wounded under mortar fire at Fossalta di Piave on July 8.

1920-   Works as a reporter and foreign correspondent for Toronto
1924   *Star* and *Star Weekly*. Meets Sherwood Anderson (1920-21), marries Hadley Richardson (1921), publishes *Three Stories and Ten Poems* in Paris (1923). Works with Ford Madox Ford on *transatlantic review*, and is friendly with Gertrude Stein and Ezra Pound. As correspondent, covers Greco-Turkish War (1922) and interviews Clemenceau and Mussolini. Publishes *in our time* in Paris (1924).

1925   Publishes *In Our Time* (Boni and Liveright) in U.S.

1926   Publishes *The Torrents of Spring* and *The Sun Also Rises* with Charles Scribner's Sons. All subsequent works except for *The Spanish Earth* will be under Scribner's imprint.

1927   Divorces Hadley Richardson; marries Pauline Pfeiffer. Publishes *Men Without Women*.

1928-   Sets up housekeeping at Key West, Florida; this home
1938   becomes the base of his various peregrinations. Begins the hobby of sports-fishing on Gulf Stream.

1929   Publishes *A Farewell to Arms*, his first major commercial success.

1930   Hurt in automobile accident in Montana.

1932   Publishes *Death in the Afternoon*.

1933-   Publishes *Winner Take Nothing* (1933). Makes first safari
1934   to Africa; also visits Paris and Spain.

1935   Publishes *Green Hills of Africa*.

1936-   Covers the Spanish Civil War for the North American
1938   Newspaper Alliance. Publishes *To Have and Have Not* (1937); helps in preparation of the film, *The Spanish Earth* (published in 1938); and issues *The Fifth Column and the First Forty-Nine Stories* (1938).

1940   Divorced by Pauline Pfeiffer; marries Martha Gelhorn. Publishes *For Whom the Bell Tolls.*

1942-   War correspondent in Europe, flies with the Royal Air
1945   Force, participates in Normandy invasion, fights his own private war to liberate Paris, and attaches himself to the Fourth Infantry Division. Is divorced from Martha Gelhorn to marry Mary Welsh in 1944.

1950   Publishes *Across the River and Into the Trees.*

1952   Publishes *The Old Man and the Sea.*

1953-   Revisits Africa; suffers two airplane crashes; is reported
1954   dead in the world press. Receives the Nobel Prize for Literature in 1954.

1961   Found dead of self-inflicted wounds at his home in Ketchum, Idaho, on July 2.

Ernest Hemingway

CHAPTER 1

The Juggler and His Masks

THE PRAGMATIC CODE of Johnson J. Hooper's great rogue-creation, Simon Suggs, was crystallized in his favorite ethical motto: "IT IS BEST TO BE SHIFTY IN A NEW COUNTRY."[1] The life, the work, and perhaps even the self-inflicted death of Ernest Hemingway may be viewed as an extended twentieth-century adaptation of Suggs's comically conceived stance against the world. But where Simon Suggs practiced shiftiness in order to exploit and victimize, Hemingway seems to have learned the Suggs attitude as a desperate means of survival. The new country that Hemingway was born into was global in extent, riven by wars, civic and domestic violence and mercurial changes in loyalties and in definitions of right conduct. Stability in such a country was the ineluctable mark of "the sitting duck"—of the grotesque parade of "potted" German soldiers who follow one another in regular cadence over the garden wall at Mons.

Stability also meant the fixed virtues of Oak Park, Illinois, or of the Oklahoma town to which Krebs returns ("Soldier's Home") after World War I. "But the world they were in," Krebs realizes, "was not the world he was in." When his mother tells him that "God has some work for every one to do" and that "there can be no idle hands in His Kingdom," Krebs must voice the deepest truth that he knows: "'I'm not in His Kingdom,' Krebs said." Hemingway's life, a romantic series of evasive actions with stop-overs at such places as Kansas City, Fossalta di Piave, Toronto, Paris, Pamplona, Key West, Nairobi, Madrid, Havana, Venice and Ketchum, Idaho, took place in a continually new, or other country; and his art is the record of his gradually improvised techniques of defense and temporary survival in that always changing and always dangerous country which is not in His Kingdom.

Hence the multiple masks which Hemingway exuberantly offered to the world; hence also the bewildering sleight of hand with which he juggled the images of Hemingway the man, the artist, the public personality, and the legend. He was the limping twenty-one-year-old ex-*Tenente* Ernesto Hemingway, recipient of the *Medaglia d'Argento al Valore* and the *Croce ad Merito di Guerra,* who had 237 pieces of shell fragment taken from his leg; the Richard Harding Davis war correspondent covering the Greco-Turkish war and sending back dispatches on the massive refugee evacuation across the Maritza River; the shy young man with "passionately interested" eyes who studied the craft of writing with Gertrude Stein and Ezra Pound and helped Ford Madox Ford edit the *transatlantic review.* He was the "spokesman" of The Lost Generation whose two volumes of short stories (*In Our Time* and *Men Without Women*) and two novels (*The Sun Also Rises* and *A Farewell to Arms*) fixed the accents of two generations into a theatrical clipped dialogue of understatement, and created a prose instrument which was later to be praised by the Nobel Prize Committee for its "forceful and style-making mastery of the art of modern narration." He was the bullfight *aficionado,* the skier, the big and little game hunter, the fisherman, the prize-fighter and shadow-boxer, the short-time darling of the Loyalist sympathizers in the Spanish Civil War, the bearded soldier of fortune miraculously transported through time to ride missions with the Royal Air Force, to land in Normandy on Fox Green Beach, to liberate Paris ahead of the columns of General Leclerc, and to fight with the Fourth Infantry Division from the Schnee-Eifel operation to the Huertgen Forest. He was the Santa Claus figure of *Field and Stream* who survived two airplane crashes in Uganda in 1954 to be able to sneer at his own obituaries which intimated that they had been expecting his death for a long time; and he was the sad-eyed isolate figure whose self-inflicted death on July 2, 1961, in Ketchum, Idaho, shocked a world that may have been expecting his death for a long time, but couldn't believe it when it actually happened.

Hemingway's biography is, of course, as yet unwritten;[2] but, when all the documents and reminiscences are collected and collated, the enigma of the man will doubtless remain. Although he was the most autobiographical of writers,[3] obsessively concerned with himself and with his own experiences in a way which brings Whitman inescapably to mind, he is—like Whitman

—wonderfully hidden in the midst of his own creation. He is so many men and so many personalities, each sharply etched and wonderfully consistent, that the total *dramatis personae* of his own charactermaking suggests that the actual man, Hemingway, is not to be found in the sum of his images, but rather in the hidden center. For each image was undeniably a true one. There was the almost ascetic apprentice to the trade of letters whom John Peale Bishop found in Montparnasse in 1922 with an "innate and genial honesty which is the very chastity of talent."[4] The Hemingway of "the loose disquisitions, arrogant, belligerent and boastful," Edmund Wilson excoriated as "the worst-invented character to be found in the author's work;"[5] this image projects a shadow of itself in *The Torrents of Spring*, makes a full appearance in *Death in the Afternoon* and in *Green Hills of Africa*, and then returns with a noisy vengeance in Lillian Ross's *New Yorker* Profile[6] and in *Across the River and Into the Trees*. The Hemingway of the Spanish Civil War, "big and lumbering, with the look of a worried boy on his round face," whom Arturo Barea describes in Madrid in 1937,[7] is as valid a *persona* as the intrepid, swashbuckling Hemingway who risked his life daily in the filming of *The Spanish Earth* and who presided nightly over the carefree parties in his shelled hotel room in the Hotel Florida (see *The Fifth Column*).

Hemingway was at times all of these figures and more. He was a craftsman dedicated to the art of letters who rarely wavered in his adherence to the highest standards of artistic probity and who significantly influenced twentieth-century writing on all levels through his aesthetic pronouncements and the principles of professionalism which he introduced and lived.[8] But he was also a night-club roisterer; a slick and chromatically unreal advertisement in the rotogravures; unfailingly "good copy" for the gossip columnists; public brawler and braggart;[9] and the "batter'd, wreck'd old man" who appeared to Seymour Betsky and Leslie Fiedler in November, 1960, as "an unsure schoolboy," desperately uncertain and frail.[10]

It would be easily possible to multiply almost endlessly the paradoxes of Hemingway's biographical identity. Born into an upper-middle class *milieu* which seems almost a caricature of late nineteenth-century Protestant respectability and conventionality,[11] he singlehandedly revivified the Byronic stereotype of the artist-adventurer. The foremost publicizer of metaphysical *nada* in our time, consistently preaching the importance of determining values on the basis of one's honest empirical experience, he converted to Roman Catholicism after the Italian campaign in World War I, and referred to himself for the rest of his life as "a rotten Catholic." Although we are told that he regarded the end of a marriage as a personal defeat,[12] he married four times—and each time to a Midwestern American girl, who was seemingly quite unlike the docile European heroines whom he and Hollywood made famous through his fictions.[13] The outstanding advocate of contempt for such obscene words as "glory, honor, courage, and sacrifice,"[14] his novel on the Spanish Civil War unashamedly rests on the very basis of "glorious sacrifice" which is implied in the title quotation (*For Whom the Bell Tolls*). An insatiable student of literature and painting, the anti-intellectualistic bias of his temperament made him a most usable proponent for the vulgar anti-intellectual position.[15] This list could be prolonged interminably, but without adding substantially to the multiple confusions which radiate from an attempt to locate the coordinates of Hemingway's character. A giant in twentieth-century literature, he can be made to seem a pygmy in many aspects of his blustering, adolescent career. And, conversely, a carefully angled study of his life and works can make him seem "the dumb ox" of letters[16] and a paragon of courage and generosity in his nonliterary life.[17]

And yet, in a curious sense, Hemingway's life and work is of a single piece, possessing total human congruity within which is encompassed the remarkable poses, the paradoxes, the violent shifts in attitude. His response to the terrors and uncertainties which contemporary life appeared to be on the verge of launching against him was the aggressive defense of guerrilla warfare—a ruthless behind-the-lines infiltration, ambush, espionage, and counterespionage. If it is best to be shifty in a new country, it is also possible to become practically invisible there by projecting so many contradictory images of one's self that one can ultimately become concealed in the center. We are reminded of the practice of dispatching surrogate kings to feudal battlefields so that the enemy might exhaust itself on their armor. And for Hemingway, fiercely competitive in everything he did, all that was not himself (animals, terrain, weather, other people, Nature, life itself) and some things, indeed, that were himself (his ambition, his talents, his ineffaceable tenderness and sensitivity, his sadistic and even his sensual desires) were potentially or actually of the enemy camp.

Although he does not formally codify the irreconcilable conflict until *A Farewell to Arms* (1929), this view is foundational in his writings from July 8, 1918 (the date of his first wound),[18] and it is retrospective from that to the memories of his earliest childhood.[19]

> If people bring so much courage to this world the world has to kill them to break them, so of course it kills them. The world breaks every one and afterward many are strong at the broken places. But those that will not break it kills. It kills the very good and the very gentle and the very brave impartially. If you are none of these you can be sure it will kill you, too, but there will be no special hurry (*Farewell*, 267).

W. M. Frohock points up this overwhelming sense of hostile isolation as a cardinal element in Hemingway's work, as follows: "From the beginning he has been concerned less with the relations between human beings than with the relations between himself, or some projection of himself, and a harsh and mainly alien universe in which violence, suffering, and death are the rule, and which, in terms of what the human being expects of it, stubbornly refuses to make sense."[20] This *donnée* of unappeasable isolation was to shape his art as thoroughly as it shaped the direction of his life and personality, but we must reserve discussion of the former for Chapter II and concentrate for the moment on the man with the many masks.

Implicit in the quoted passage from *A Farewell to Arms* is the controlling metaphor of the game, or the contest: "The world breaks every one and afterward many are strong at the broken places. But those that will not break it kills." This statement would seem to make it beholden for man to learn how to be broken that he may mend himself for his savage encounter with the world. This also suggests that there are some rules that guide the contest, ruthless and unjust as it may be: "You did not know what it was about. You never had time to learn. They threw you in and told you the rules and the first time they caught you off base they killed you."[21] The epigraph which Hemingway himself wrote for his volume of short stories, *Winner Take Nothing* (1932),[22] develops the game metaphor further: "Unlike all other forms of lutte or combat the conditions are that the winner shall take nothing; neither his ease, nor his pleasure, nor any notions of glory; nor, if he win far enough, shall there be any reward within himself."

A year earlier, in *Death in the Afternoon,* he had described the significant difference between the *suertes* of a good bull-fighter and those that were without emotion and relevance:

> It is the difference between playing cards with an individual who, giving no importance to the game and having no sum at stake, gives no attention to the rules and makes the game impossible and one who having learned the rules, through having them forced on him and through losing; and now, having his fortune and life at stake, gives much importance to the game and the rules, finding them forced upon him, and does his best with utmost seriousness. It is up to the bullfighter to make the bull play and to enforce the rules. The bull has no desire to play, only to kill. (147)

From 1918 until the end of his life (and also probably long before 1918), Hemingway gave his utmost concentration to the rules, playing his game for survival with all the means at his disposal. His rootlessness is a matter of public legend; freed from the financial necessity of holding a regular job by the commercial success of *A Farewell to Arms,* he and his retinue roamed through four continents—to the delight of the photographers—in search of excitement and new sensations, but also in order to keep from being trapped in one place.[23]

His record of unsuccessful marriages and his often violently shattered friendships (particularly with Sherwood Anderson and Gertrude Stein),[24] as well as his occasionally unprovoked attacks on relatively harmless individuals,[25] project a picture of a man hypersensitively ready to strike out against a potential foe before he himself is struck. And it may be significant that, in all of his fiction, Hemingway—who is, after all, our modern poet of camaraderie—nowhere depicts a really mutual friendship. The closest is perhaps between Frederick Henry and Rinaldi in *A Farewell to Arms,* but even there the two characters move through their own self-propelled orbits; they share little except wine and bright conversation. The pattern is similar between Jake Barnes and Bill Gorton of *The Sun Also Rises;* and, although some of the later fictions chronicle with delicacy a relationship of mutual *respect* between persons (Robert Jordan and Anselmo, especially), the evidence suggests that Hemingway was not a man inclined to expose himself to the trust that friendship requires.[26]

In this context his notorious female characterizations ("There isn't any me. I'm you. Don't make up a separate me.") in which the beloved is totally subservient to the intermittent desires of the lover offer added evidence. A love affair can conceivably expose the man to the shock of his partner's impregnating personality; for this to happen, however, there must be at least a relaxing of the taut barriers with which the male protects his inmost self. Hemingway's lovers—Frederick Henry, Harry Morgan, Robert Jordan, Philip Rawlings, Richard Cantwell—are genuinely moved by the pleasure and devotion which their respective sweethearts generously proffer upon them; they are profoundly disturbed by the impersonal malice of life in those instances where death or duty put abrupt ends to their happy affairs; but in no case does the private circle of their most personal experience of themselves seem seriously affected.[27] They all seem to have taken strongly to heart the advice of the Major of "In Another Country" that a man must not marry: "He should not place himself in a position to lose. He should find things he cannot lose."

It is not surprising, therefore, that Hemingway's instinctual need to defend himself in a hostile world and his device of multiple personality-screens should lead to the creation of a series of images—personal, fictional, and legendary—which would have a profound appeal for his fellow writers and his readers between 1926 and 1941. The mood which marked the 1920's of expatriation and alienation, of massive disillusionment with traditional values of all kinds, of deep-rooted distrust with any sort of collective venture was a tailor-made situation for the young romantic iconoclast who was learning to write above a carpenter shop in the rue de Notre Dame des Champs.[28] He had certain distinct personal advantages to offer: he was attractive, athletic, and quick to learn languages; his journalistic background and his instinctive concern with how things work gave him at least the appearance of the insider's *expertise* in a foreign situation; he had the bizarre experience of having served, been wounded, and decorated in a foreign army. And his rebellion against the conventional *mores* of American rural-and-village life patterns antedated the disenchantment of World War I. (Hemingway had run away from home several times while in high school; and, of course, he had never attended college.)

On top of this he was patently teaching himself the craft of fiction. Working with Gertrude Stein and Ezra Pound and with the horrors of his own experience, Hemingway was carving out a prose style which would be (in Ford Madox Ford's phrase) as new and clean as "pebbles fresh from a brook."[29] It is not surprising, therefore, that such contemporaries as Edmund Wilson, John Peale Bishop, and F. Scott Fitzgerald should see in the Hemingway of 1925 a potential new Moses (or at least a Joshua) who might lead American art out of the arid deserts of the nineteenth century into a Promised Land beyond imagining.

The images and texture of his fiction also insured him a favorable reception with the reading audiences of the 1920's and 1930's. His prose was fast and violent enough to make excellent barbershop reading; his dialogue—especially in *The Sun Also Rises*—was sophisticatedly clever enough to recall the balmy days of *The Smart Set.* There was the delight of a well-told action story with sensationalism and forbidden sex for the common reader; for the uncommon reader there was the discovery of a new aesthetic for approaching literature and evaluating life. With the publication of *A Farewell to Arms* Hemingway's reading audience was secured, and it remained only for him to maintain a supply of new material for its consumption.[30] For we must remember that Hemingway's immense popularity during his lifetime took place on two distinct levels. From the October, 1924, *Dial* review of *In Our Time*[31] to the *Life* magazine installments of *The Dangerous Summer,*[32] Hemingway's work was subject to constant critical evaluation and appreciation on the most serious levels even as it was lustily consumed by an unsophisticated mass-audience.[33] No other serious writer of Hemingway's stature in the twentieth century commanded as large and as responsive a readership *through all levels of society* as he did.

Several speculations beyond the obvious may be offered to suggest the reasons for Hemingway's mass popularity through the 1930's which continued with *For Whom the Bell Tolls* (1940) and with *The Old Man and the Sea* (1952). The psychological effects of the world-wide depression of the 1930's are far too complicated to trace in detail, but surely one effect of the massive economic paralysis of the times was a strengthening of the total bureaucratization of life and an increasing sense (individually felt) of the impotence and helplessness of the single unit, man. The traditional notion of the possibilities of *heroism*—in the capacity of man to front the world with a certain degree of success, using only the powers and resources that were his own natural inheritance—this concept of heroism had almost disappeared in serious fiction. Readers were invited to identify with heroes who were bewildered, frustrated victims of one sort or another—Leopold Bloom, Joseph K.—or with heroes who were unsuccessful, broken rebels—Jay Gatsby, Joe Christmas.

Hemingway was, as Sean O'Faolain said, "the only modern writer of real distinction for whom the Hero does in some form still live."[34] It should not be necessary to belabor this point at this time, and even though Hemingway's heroes are in a sense, winners who take nothing, they *are* winners and the manner of their taking is individually self-generated, within situations largely of their own choosing, and under circumstances in which their native resources for physical action and courage are given every possibility of expression. The radical significance of the individual as an important integer in the struggle for existence, largely denied or neglected in the fiction of the 1920's and 1930's, is a salient first factor in Hemingway's mass popularity.

A second and related reason for his popularity may well be the vicarious excitement of physical and sensuous experience that Hemingway offered in abundance to an audience increasingly urban-oriented, increasingly desensitized and immunized from a physical life of full sensory response.[35] Hemingway's talent for evoking physical sensations, for transmuting into prose how it is to *taste,* to *see,* to *hear,* to *smell,* to *feel* in a great variety of ways is a staple ingredient of his prose. And these sensations are typically presented within a framework of physical or psycholog-ical stress, in which the narrative perspective is left open-ended so that the attentive reader is forced to serve as the "ground" for the powerful prose-currents of the presented action. That is, the sensations are not merely described, but presented within a controlled frame of dramatic awareness, and the reader is invited to participate in, as well as to observe, the bombardment of sensory stimuli. The effect of the prose on this level is a cumula-tive one, but perhaps the following short passage from "Big Two-Hearted River: Part II" may give a partial demonstration of this involvement:

> On the left, where the meadow ended and the woods began, a great elm tree was uprooted. Gone over in a storm, it lay back into the woods, its roots clotted with dirt, grass growing in them, rising a solid bank beside the stream. The river cut to the edge of the uprooted tree. From where Nick stood he could see deep channels, like ruts, cut in the shallow bed of the stream

by the flow of the current. Pebbly where he stood and pebbly and full of boulders beyond; where it curved near the tree roots, the bed of the stream was marly and between the ruts of deep water green weed fronds swung in the current.

The Hemingway protagonist, like Nick in this excerpt, is actively engaged in some form of purposive activity; and the reader has no choice except to join him in the activity. At the same time, the activity of the protagonist takes place within an ambience of external activity: the grass is *actively growing*, the stream is *actively* running, the weed fronds are *actively swinging*, etc. If it is possible for prose to coerce vicarious sensory response at all, Hemingway's prose, with its intense concentration on action and *active* response, is admirably suited to secure such an effect.[36]

And finally, in addition to these factors, Hemingway the public personality (who gradually merges into Hemingway the legend) becomes an additional contributing element to excite the unparalleled avidity with which his stories and even his casual remarks were received. Hemingway became for a great number of readers not only the describer of heroism and physical activity but also the actual hero himself. His exploits in all forms of sport—and later his military activities—were duly recorded, improved upon, and ground out in the publicity mills of the world press. It is actually irrelevant that the largest part of his alleged achievements have been factually corroborated; the point is that the public life of the writer overwhelmed his writings and re-entered his prose as a substantiating force for the aesthetic validity of those works. In the case of no other serious American writer except Mark Twain and Walt Whitman had the writer's personality become such an intrusive and confusing factor in the judgment and reception of his works.[37] A cursory examination of the criticism which is primarily directed against or in defense of the reputed Hemingway personality will give ample evidence of the confusions to which literary critics are quite justifiably susceptible.[38]

But if this consequence was a source of frustration and impediment to a dispassionate evaluation of Hemingway's works, it was also a final stimulus for his commercial popularity. The distinction between life and literature tended, in his case, to blur and merge. Reading Hemingway was as informative as reading the newspapers, and much more exciting. And the vision of heroism, the proof that the individual could still wage

solitary battle against the elemental forces that oppress mankind, could be found not only in the breezy, tight-lipped dispatches which the legendary Hemingway sent back to *Collier's*,
to *Ken*, or to *Esquire*, but also in the strained expressions of
grim grandeur with which Gary Cooper sighted along the barrel
of his machine gun at the Fascist cavalry lieutenant, or with
which Spencer Tracy reeled in the big marlin.

Meanwhile there was an actual flesh-and-blood Hemingway
behind all the masks. The poses, the shiftings of personality, the
sporadic outbursts of frightened aggressiveness were the means
through which Hemingway the man might survive, might fore-
stall the destruction which he felt awaited American writers.
But merely to survive was not enough. The rules of the game
called for total competition—unconditional surrender on one
side or the other. And the weapon that Hemingway selected—
the weapon that all his personality machinations were designed
to protect—was his capacity to create art: "A country, finally,
erodes and the dust blows away, the people all die and none
of them were of any importance permanently, except those who
practised the arts. . . . A thousand years makes economics silly
and a work of art endures forever. . . ."[39] To write a prose with
"nothing that will go bad afterwards" would be to achieve
importance; to secure a small piece of almost tangible immortality; to gain a handsome victory over life in which, even
though the winner takes nothing for himself, the mere survival
is made to yield a product that will endure forever.

Undisputed champion in 1929, Hemingway's publications of
the next decade did little to increase his literary stature. Except
for a half dozen short stories, his volumes of the 1930's were
generally inferior productions. Although *Death in the Afternoon*
(1932) can be defended on special grounds and although
interesting things can be found in *Green Hills of Africa* (1935),
it was difficult for even his fiercest partisans to find much to
applaud in *To Have and Have Not* (1937) or *The Fifth Column*
(1938). On top of this, the chilly winds of social and political
doctrines had virtually dispelled the pleasant *laissez-faire* airs
of aestheticism which had nurtured Hemingway's original emergence into the literary scene in the 1920's.[40] The lone-wolf
Hemingway hero and the lone-wolf Hemingway, hunting luxu-
riously in Africa and Wyoming and fishing the Gulf Stream
for sport while millions were unemployed and the world seemed
to be organizing itself toward total collapse, were not palatable

images for many critics and intellectuals of the mid-1930's, although it is doubtful that the common reader was disturbed. Hemingway's partial renunciation of "the separate peace" in his decision to go to Spain and his publication of *For Whom the Bell Tolls* (1940), followed by the war years (1941-45), gave a temporary surcease to the critics and probably also to Hemingway's struggles for immortality.

But the game he had elected to play was a relentless one. Santiago, in *The Old Man and the Sea*, could very well be speaking for his author as he describes his attitude in the face of the new encounter: "The thousand times that he had proved it meant nothing. Now he was proving it again. Each time was a new time and he never thought about the past when he was doing it." Nor was there any possibility for Hemingway to avoid the new encounters; to live meant to struggle with all that was not himself, and this in turn required him to write continually a prose that would not go bad. It is hard for us to believe that he could have judged *Across the River and Into the Trees* (1950) to be superior to *A Farewell to Arms*.[41] And we wonder whether his statement to the Nobel Prize Committee that "it is because we have had such great writers in the past that a writer is driven far out past where he can go, out to where no one can help him,"[42] is either literary cliché or the proclamation of a terrifying desperation and loneliness. My own notion would hold the latter to be true since it yields some explanation of the last seven years of Hemingway life. The magic capacity to turn out prose would seem to have gone bad;[43] and, with the collapse of the ultimate weapon against life, the ironic control over the masks and poses must have been lost.

We will probably never know what the last years of Hemingway's life were like; he who was so careful to guard his inmost privacy during his flourishing times would not be prone to expose himself in his hurt. It would be fair to suggest, however, that they were years of a very special kind of agony, and it is also fair to presume that Hemingway was brave under the agony.[45] And although it is inexcusably arrogant to theorize on such matters, it is possible to find his death predictable and in keeping with the total pattern of his life. All readers of Hemingway know his special concern with suicide (his father had shot himself in 1928) which provides a theme for "Fathers and Sons" and an undercurrent for Robert Jordan's reminiscences in *For Whom the Bell Tolls*. Suicide appears in most of Hemingway's works as a complete abrogation of the rules of the game. It is even worse than dying badly, which, is in accordance, at least, with the rules. His views on death were rather aggressively expounded to Lillian Ross in May, 1950:

> . . . I'll make the prettiest corpse since Pretty Boy Floyd. Only suckers worry about saving their souls. Who the hell should care about saving his soul when it's a man's duty to lose it intelligently, the way you would sell a position you were defending, if you could not hold it, as expensively as possible, trying to make it the most expensive position that was ever sold. It isn't hard to die. . . . No more worries. . . . It takes a pretty good man to make any sense when he's dying.[44]

Perhaps it is just to assume that Hemingway's death was his way of *selling a position* that could no longer be held, and that for him this was the most intelligent way to handle the necessary transaction. Having chosen to do battle with nothing less than eternity on a day-to-day basis, it may have been his way of complying with the rules insofar as the rules required the unconditional surrender of one of the combatants. It is also possible that his death was Hemingway's calculated punishment of that aspect of himself which had failed him in his need. Just as his creativity had been his prime resource in the struggle for a small piece of immortality, so death would strike with unerring accuracy at the part that had offended—at the creativity itself. And finally, without negating these two possibilities, there is always the chance that his death was Hemingway's final act of personality prestidigitation. The master juggler, in danger of having his whole spinning world fall in shambles at his feet—himself naked and powerless to control—could in one final manipulation of a new mask put a triumphant crown to his whole glittering career. These are, of course, unfounded speculations, but there is no need to assume that Hemingway was any less shifty in the new country that he left, than he was when he entered. Nor is it idle sentimentality to suppose that if any man could make sense—in Hemingway's terms—when he was dying, it would be Hemingway himself.

CHAPTER 2

The Real Thing

I

IN THE preceding chapter we noticed that the act of writing performed at least two functions for Hemingway: it was his weapon against an alien universe—the means by which he kept himself alive; and it was the battlefield in which he struggled for a small piece of immortality. Both of these are very good personal reasons why a man should become a writer, and both have long and respectable antecedents in the history of literature.[1] But neither reason throws much illumination on the underlying principles which govern Hemingway's typical artistic approach and technique. These reasons have relevance solely to Hemingway, but they suggest no connection between Hemingway and the rest of the world.

If we can discover what it is that he intends his fictions to accomplish—what it is that they must do to be "right"—we will be in a better position to examine and properly judge the results. And Hemingway has been characteristically both forthright and deceptive in his statements about his artistic purposes; he has stated frequently and positively that he is concerned with capturing "truth," with transcribing accurately "the way it was." "Let those who want to save the world if you can get to see it clear and as a whole. Then any part you make will represent the whole if it's made truly."[2] His statements have an impressive authoritarian ring, but "truth"—one of Hemingway's favorite words—is a protean entity in a metaphysic founded on incessant conflict where the winner takes nothing. It may, then, be more sensible to approach Hemingway's aesthetic from a roundabout direction and to ignore for the moment his excessive protestations of the "true."

The Real Thing

As a starting point we may note that Hemingway's consistent test for the authenticity of an art object is the involuntary subjective response of the perceiver. When Robert Jordan in *For Whom the Bell Tolls* (225) repeats to himself the dying speech of Maria's mother, "He knew it was good because it made a tingle run all over him when he said it to himself." Similarly, watching his first bullfight before he had trained himself to discriminate between good and bad bulls, or good and bad bullfighters, Hemingway recalls being profoundly moved by the kill: "I remembered in the midst of this confused excitement having a great moment of emotion when the man went in with the sword." He is careful to point out that it was not just the act of killing, but the properly administered (aesthetically correct) act of killing that caused his emotion, since he watched the slaughter of some fifty more bulls before this emotion was elicited again.[3] It is perhaps relevant to note that at late as 1954, Hemingway subjected his writing to the same kinetic test; if his writing raised gooseflesh on Miss Mary's (his wife's) arms, he knew it must be good.[4] I suppose all artists invoke some variety of kinetic test, but Hemingway seems to have taken this more seriously than most—seems, indeed, to have made the stimulation of an emotion in the reader a cardinal point in his aesthetic. The consequences of this—the primacy of *feelings* in his notion of morality as well as art—will become obvious and far-reaching.

The first effect is to give the artist a special role in human affairs, a role which will separate him from his audience as decisively as the *barrera* separates the paying spectators from the brave matador. And given Hemingway's temperamental obsession with himself and his insatiate need to be an "insider," a professional who performs rather than a customer who watches, this separation between artist and audience has a strong tendency to turn into a competition between them and, indeed, to become even an assault in which the artist has all the good cards in his hands. It is difficult to discuss this concept without overstating the case; but, if we overstate it now for the sake of clarity, we can make the proper redresses later. Typically Hemingway will use the metaphors of games, sports, bullfights, and wars to describe his views on life. The Passion of Christ is described within the values of prizefighting terminology ("Today Is Friday"), as is the prowess of military leaders and great artists. Baseball, football, horse-racing, hunting, and fishing provide him with his consistent metaphors for expression.[5] But the significance of this use goes deeper than colorful atmosphere and than the often-noted aggressive competitiveness that marked Hemingway's literary and non-literary career. The metaphor of violent games provided Hemingway with a structure in which he could cast his aesthetic—present again and again his portraits of the artist as hunter, fisherman, matador, soldier, prize fighter, and gambler.

One of the few extraneous scenes in *The Sun Also Rises*—and, at the same time, a passage which seems to be so honestly felt that it obtrudes from the carefully controlled "theatricalness" of the main narrative—concerns itself with the appearance of Juan Belmonte in the Pamplona bull ring. Belmonte has returned from retirement, sick and forced to battle the legend of his former prowess as well as the bulls:

> . . . the public, who wanted three times as much from Belmonte, who was sick with a fistula, as Belmonte had ever been able to give, felt defrauded and cheated, and Belmonte's jaw came further out in contempt, and his face turned yellower, and he moved with greater difficulty as his pain increased, and finally the crowd were actively against him, and he was utterly contemptuous and indifferent. He had meant to have a great afternoon, and instead it was an afternoon of sneers, shouted insults, and finally a volley of cushions and pieces of bread and vegetables, thrown down at him in the plaza where he had had his greatest triumphs. His jaw only went further out. Sometimes he turned to smile that toothed, long-jawed, lipless smile when he was called something particularly insulting, and always the pain that any movement produced grew stronger and stronger, until finally his yellow face was parchment color, and after his second bull was dead and the throwing of bread and cushions was over, after he had saluted the President with the same wolf-jawed smile and contemptuous eyes, and handed his sword over the barrera to be wiped, and put back in its case, he passed through into the callejon and leaned on the barrera below us, his head on his arms, not seeing, not hearing anything, only going through his pain. When he looked up, finally, he asked for a drink of water. He swallowed a little, rinsed his mouth, spat the water, took his cape, and went back into the ring (222-23).

Hemingway seems to have felt the significance of this scene so strongly that he was unable to eradicate it from the narrative where it serves only as a contrasting foil for Pedro Romero's success.[6] The centrality of this image to his thinking can be seen when we remember how many of his heroes are winners who perform valiantly only to have their prizes taken away or scorned. Manuel of "The Undefeated" has the same contempt and indifference for the crowd as Belmonte does, and suffers even greater disdain. Francis Macomber stands before the charge of the buffalo in perfect accord with the hunting code; and his wife—the *only* nonprofessional observer—rewards him by blasting out his brains. Richard Cantwell (*Across the River and Into the Trees*) makes a career of being a good soldier and is deranked from the General Staff as a result. And Santiago lands the biggest marlin in the history of literature only to lose it, piece by piece, to the voracious sharks.

The portrait of the artist that begins to emerge is that of the individual, compelled by his special talents, or sensitivities, or hurts (and at times, Hemingway would seem to equate all three), to accept life as a kind of game. This he (the artist-player) does not choose to do, if he is a serious player; the choice is forced upon him:

> It is a vast wheel, set at an angle, and each time it goes around and then is back to where it starts. One side is higher than the other and the sweep it makes lifts you back and down to where you started. There are no prizes either, he thought, and no one would choose to ride this wheel. You ride it each time and make the turn with no intention ever to have mounted. There is only one turn; one large, elliptical, rising and falling turn and you are back where you have started (*For Whom the Bell Tolls*, 225).

Once he has made his commitment to the game, however, the contract is eternally binding; he is arbitrarily defined in the universe as a bullfighter (like Manuel), as a fisherman (like Santiago), as a soldier (like Cantwell), as a writer like Hemingway. The rules of the game require that he learn his trade as swiftly and thoroughly as possible, that he strive to be better at his craft than anyone has ever been, and that he have a deep humility and respect for the materials within and against which he must practice his craft. These materials would include bulls, marlins and the sea, opposing soldiers and the terrain on which battles must be fought, wild game, words, and one's experience of the past. Nothing else, himself included, is worthy of respect.

But the conflict rarely takes place in a social vacuum. Conceivably a matador could fight bulls without an audience, even as a hunter or a fisherman goes off to the woods alone to exercise his sporting talents. Conceivably, also, a writer can wrestle with language and float his results on pieces of rice paper down the nearest river. But such a writer would have to possess a very secure sense of *oneness* with the universe—precisely that sense which we have seen to be severely lacking in Hemingway's orientation. Thus the composite portrait of Hemingway's artist requires an audience in order that the poetic execution of the craft can be made in some sense permanent. Let us return to *Death in the Afternoon* which serves in so many ways as Hemingway's *Principles of Poetic Composition*:

> It is impossible to believe the emotional and spiritual intensity and pure, classic beauty that can be produced by a man, an animal and a piece of scarlet serge draped over a stick. If you do not choose to believe it possible and want to regard it all as nonsense you may be able to prove you are right by going to a bullfight in which nothing magical occurs. . . . But if you should ever see the real thing you would know it. It is an experience that either you will have in your life or you will never have. . . . But if you ever do see one, finished by a great estocada, you will know it and there will be many things you will forget before it will be gone (207).

Again we find the touchstone of the kinetic experience—the something "magical" that occurs in the successful performance of an art. This is made more definite in a succeeding passage:

> Now the essence of the greatest emotional appeal of bullfighting is the feeling of immortality that the bullfighter feels in the middle of a great faena and that he gives to the spectators. He is performing a work of art and he is playing with death, bringing it closer, closer, closer, to himself, a death that you know is in the horns because you have the canvas-covered bodies of the horses on the sand to prove it. He gives the feeling of his immortality, and, as you watch it, it becomes yours. Then when it belongs to both of you, he proves it with the sword (213).

This, then, is the ideal Hemingway artist—the man who in the midst of a great *faena* makes an imperishable poem of his own body and patterned gestures, who achieves immortality through the perfection of his controlled dance with death, and who has so well educated or sensitized his audience that he can allow them to share in the immortality that he has created.

This is the ideal portrait of the artist for Hemingway, but even as an ideal it has serious deficiencies for him. The bull-fight takes place *in time* and the feeling of immortality is communicated *in time*. And although he suggests optimistically that "there will be many things you will forget before it will be gone," it is inevitable that it too will be forgotten, or falsified by memory. Thus his first problem is to discover a medium—"a fourth and fifth dimension" in prose—which will hold the emotion of immortality. Then there is the second problem of the audience. In the ideal portrait, the audience is composed entirely of *aficionados* like Hemingway; in actual practice—both in bull rings and among reading audiences—the spectators are not worthy to share The Host. They are uninformed, or uninvolved, or too calloused and cynical to be receptive to mysteries. Further, they can easily become antagonistic to the artist; they will try to sap his strength and to bribe him away from the integrity of his dedication through the classic temptations of wealth, power, sex, or easy indolence. The actual audience is the great enemy for the artist because without it he is consigned to an endless narcissistic exhibitionism; but with it he is always in danger of being dragged down to its seamy, time-serving level. And the third problem with the ideal portrait is the difficulty of persuading one's self or one's audience that the artist "is playing with death, bringing it closer, closer, closer, to himself" when he is merely tapping typewriter keys or writing in longhand while he stands up to a writing-table.[7] Hemingway's efforts to solve these deficiencies, or to learn to live with them, should explain the development of his aesthetic.

II

Before we attempt to describe this development, we must first examine Hemingway's one careful presentation of a *non-ideal* portrait of an artist; for against this we may test our perceptions. Although many of Hemingway's heroes might nominally qualify as artists—Jake Barnes, writer; Nick Adams, writer; Frederick Henry, architect; Richard Cantwell, expert in general; Robert Jordan, writer—only Harry of "The Snows of Kilimanjaro" is presented convincingly as a writer; and only he seems actively concerned with the problems created by his calling.[8] Structurally the story is rather simple—a variation on Ambrose Bierce's classic "An Occurrence at Owl Creek Bridge."

Harry, the writer, tries to come to terms with the fact of his approaching death; he has a badly gangrenous leg which is too far advanced to be cured, even though a rescue airplane is expected on the following day to carry him out of the African bush to the nearest hospital. He spends the afternoon and early evening quarreling with his wealthy wife, berating himself for having wasted his talents, remembering sharp vignettes of the past that he had always intended to use in his writing but never did. The last section of the story (as in Bierce's model) is a description of the arrival of the airplane and its ascent to the top of Kilimanjaro: "great, high, and unbelievably white in the sun." Then the story flashes back to the dead Harry discovered by his wife, and we realize that the airplane ride was Hemingway's trick on the reader. The story is prefaced by the following epigraph: "Kilimanjaro is a snow-covered mountain 19,710 feet high, and is said to be the highest mountain in Africa. Its western summit is called the Masai 'Ngaje Ngai,' the House of God. Close to the western summit there is the dried and frozen carcass of a leopard. No one has explained what the leopard was seeking at that altitude."[9]

Thematically the story is also relatively simple, and it is reminiscent of Henry James's "The Middle Years" in which another writer confronts the fact of death and berates himself and life for not having time enough to write the things he is now ready to do. If we approach "The Snows of Kilimanjaro" from the special view with which we have been concerned, we will see that Hemingway used a traditional structure and a conventional theme to achieve his own peculiar ends; and we will also see that Harry is a kind of extended portrait of the artist, similar in attitude to the portrait of Belmonte previously cited.

First, there are some obvious, paired contrasts within the story: the snow, clean and cold on the mountain top and in Harry's reminiscence, as against "the heat shimmer of the plain" which becomes associated with the ugly rotting leg. Similarly, "the dried and frozen carcass" of the leopard is contrasted to the wide-snouted hyena which is the harbinger and final announcer of Harry's death. Through various devices, Helen is contrasted with Harry and associated with the heat, the plain, the gangrene, and the hyena. The contrasts are all neat and in balance, with the exception of Harry; he, of course, is connected to the leg, Helen, and the hyena—even as he dreams of the snow and the ascent beyond the plain. And it is Harry's character that provides the key to the story. He is not, at all, a nice man. He is a liar, a quarreler, and a traitor to himself as well as to other people. "He had sold vitality, in one form or another, all his life and when your affections are not too involved you give much better value for the money." He had married Helen, he tells us, for security and comfort, and he had never loved her. And yet, "it was strange . . . that he should be able to give her more for her money than when he had really loved."

Several things should be obvious. Harry is egocentric, hypocritical, and morally as well as physically rotten; and yet the thrust of values in the story elevates him to the snow-capped summit and forces the reader to accept him as a superior man. Helen, on the other hand, is honest, generous, and reasonably intelligent; yet she is left at the end of the story with the unbandaged leg that she cannot bear to look at. Harry disposes of her for himself and for the reader in one sentence: "She was always thoughtful, he thought. On anything she knew about, or had read, or that she had ever heard." On normal standards of valuation, this would seem to be generous praise; but in terms of the story, it is clear that this is enough to make Helen despicable. Harry, it would seem, is thoughtful on things he *doesn't* know about, *hasn't* read, and *hasn't ever heard*. He is justly contemptuous of artists, like Julian (F. Scott Fitzgerald), who have been wrecked. He is justly contemptuous of Helen and her total *milieu;* he is "a spy in their country" and, by implication, a mysterious stranger in all countries save that which he shares with a frozen leopard at an altitude of almost 20,000 feet. And the only source of his marvellous superiority is that "for years it [death] had obsessed him; but now it meant nothing in itself." That, and the fact that in the face of death, he performs his craft; *he writes*.[10] This is what makes him superior; this is what gives him "the feeling of immortality" which is vouchsafed to him in his ascent to the mountain.

The portrait of Harry is thus very similar to the earlier picture of Belmonte. Both are sick with disgust at their unknowing audiences (Helen is Harry's audience), but both, presumably, attain a level of inner possession which can only be called beatific. Harry differs from Belmonte in that he manages in an offhand way to satisfy his audience even with the gangrene. The remarkable *tour de force* of the story is that Hemingway is able to present a thoroughly upside-down world to readers who must not be very different from Helen—and to make them like it. And here we must mention the hyena in order to appreciate the full resonance of the *tour de force*. The hyena is introduced into the story in such a way as to connect it to the obscenely squatting vultures which sit with their "naked heads sunk in their hunched feathers," presumably waiting for Harry's death. It, like them, is called "a filthy animal" and a "bastard," and it is quickly associated with the "sudden evil-smelling emptiness" that characterizes the approach of both the gangrene and death in the narrative. But *after* Harry dies, the hyena appears again: "Just then the hyena stopped whimpering in the night and started to make a strange, human, almost crying sound." He continues to do this until Helen wakes up and discovers the corpse. If the hyena were simply meant to stand for death, its continual symbolic use is a foolish distraction which dissipates the force of the story. And why the emphasis on "human," especially since the hyena's crying is almost the first "human" sound in the story?

It is possible to suggest an interpretation for the hyena which will be in keeping with the reading of the story and the portraiture of the artist that we have been examining, if we call to mind Hemingway's description of the "highly humorous" hyena in *Green Hills of Africa*. The hyena is a source of much amusement in that book because of the obscenely funny contortions that he goes through when he is shot.

> . . . the pinnacle of hyenic humor, was the hyena, the classic hyena, that hit too far back while running, would circle madly, snapping and tearing at himself until he pulled his own intestines out, and then stood there, jerking them out and eating them with relish. . . . Fisi, the hyena, hermaphroditic, self-eating devourer of the dead, trailer of calving cows, ham-stringer, potential biter-off of your face at night while you slept, sad yowler, camp-follower, stinking, foul . . . mongrel dog-smart in the face . . . (37-38).

The despicable hyena joins Helen in weeping for the dead artist, because the hyena becomes a distended identification of the audience that the artist must serve. Fickle, treacherous, stupid and cunning at the same time, it is quick to lament the loss of the artist, even as it is quick to harry him down when he is alive. Without pushing the metaphor too far, it is fair to say that Hemingway succeeds in this story in insulting his audience beyond endurance, in making the audience eat its own wounds, and like it. There is surely a more than savage irony in the "human, almost crying sound" that ends the tale; and the reflection that Hemingway was reputed to have received $125,000 for the movie rights to this story merely compounds the irony.[11]

If this description of Hemingway's attitudes as an artist seems somewhat harsh, we should look again at the stance which Hemingway aggressively assumed against life: "You never saw a counter-puncher who was punchy. Never lead against a hitter unless you can outhit him. Crowd a boxer, and take everything he has to get inside. Duck a swing. Block a hook. And counter a jab with everything you own. Papa's delivery of hard-learned facts of life."[12]

Papa's delivery of hard-learned facts of life should teach us, then, to be chary in approaching his fictions. They will attempt to create an emotional charge of some sort, but more often than not, the charge will be exploded at the vulnerability of the unwitting reader. The success of the fiction, in part, will depend upon the author's ability to "lead" the reader, to hook him soundly, and when he is hooked and wriggling against the wall, to administer the gaff accurately and well. Many critics have noticed the tendencies of Hemingway's sporting and bull-fighting descriptions to move into areas usually connotative of the writing process:

> He looked down into the water and watched the lines that went straight down into the dark of the water. He kept them straighter than anyone did, so that at each level in the darkness of the stream there would be a bait waiting exactly where he wished it to be for any fish that swam there. Others let them drift with the current and sometimes they were at sixty fathoms when the fishermen thought they were at a hundred.
>
> But, he thought, I keep them with precision. Only I have no luck any more. But who knows? Maybe today. Every day is a new day. It is better to be lucky. But I would rather be exact. Then when luck comes you are ready (*The Old Man and the Sea*, 35-37).

We are reminded of Hemingway's evaluation of Edgar Allan Poe's work: "It is skillful, marvelously constructed, and it is dead."[13] Seemingly, then, the prose "that has never been written," the prose "without tricks and without cheating," the prose "with nothing that will go bad afterwards," will be like Poe's except that it will be *alive*. And while Hemingway was seeking this prose in the early 1920's, there was an abundance of individual writers and movements from which he could borrow, if he wanted to, and which he could easily adapt to his own ends.

III

For the sake of simplicity, I will restrict the discussion of Hemingway and the "influences" upon him to five rather arbitrarily selected areas. It should be remembered, of course, that the creation of a prose style hardly follows the mechanical principles of a cake recipe and that a writer as eagerly educable and eclectic as Hemingway is particularly unresponsive to this kind of analysis. The attempt to discuss influences is justifiable, however, in that it may give us a rough idea of what Hemingway was doing to fashion the medium that would contain "the emotional intensity" that he required and, at the same time, be subservient to the special kind of assault which seems to have been a psychological necessity for him to launch.

A major discernible influence was undoubtedly Ring Lardner's, whose exploitation of the world of the sports page and savagely ironic techniques of presentation paralleled Hemingway's interests acutely.[14] Writing for the *Trapeze* (the Oak Park High School literary paper), and later for *Ciao* (the newsletter intermittently distributed by the Red Cross Ambulance Unit in Italy, Section IV), Hemingway consciously imitated Lardner. Hemingway adapted Lardner's poker-faced, first-person narrator's mode of presentation to the area of local interests that both chatty newspapers required. Thus, in *Ciao* we find this early Hemingway:

> Well Al we are here in this old Italy and now that I am here I am not going to leave it. Not at all if any. And that is not no New Years revolution Al but the truth. Well Al I am now an officer and if you would meet me you have to salute me. What I am is a provisional acting second lieutenant without a commission but the trouble is that all the other fellows are too. There ain't no privates in our army Al and the Captain is called a chef. But he don't look to me as tho he could cook a damn bit.

Although it would be foolish to exaggerate their importance, we can find many likenesses to the kind of fiction that Hemingway was to produce in Lardner's *You Know Me, Al* collection and in his later short stories, "Haircut" and "Alibi Ike." There is a strong similarity in the mordant and sardonic attitudes of the two writers, as well as a common penchant for adopting a mask which will conceal the bitter, shocked responses of the authors to the cruelty and injustice of life. Hemingway's vignettes of violence in *in our time* and his pieces like "Mr. and Mrs. Elliot," "After the Storm," and "A Natural History of the Dead" have significant affinities with the structural devices of Lardner's fiction, which aim to evoke an overwhelming disgust with what they are innocuously presenting under a mask of naïve or ignorant acceptance. It might not even be too far out of line to suppose that Hemingway caught in Lardner's humor his own first glimpse of that "toothed, long-jawed, lipless smile" which was Belmonte's measure of contempt for the audience he was serving. We ought also to remember that Hemingway in *The Torrents of Spring* (1926), made his feeble obeisances to the ghost of Henry Fielding and that, although traditional satire was never within the control of his talents, it is almost always an ingredient of them. Thus, Hemingway could have found in Lardner an early model on which to base his experiments in colloquial speech-patterns and in modes of narrative presentation, as well as a kindred spirit in mordancy and spiritual outrage.

Another major influence in the formation of Hemingway's style was his journalistic experience on the Kansas City *Star* (1917-18) and the Toronto *Daily Star* and *Star Weekly* (1919-23).[15] It is as easy to overestimate this influence as it is to undervalue it, but certain factual observations can be made. Hemingway's seven months on the Kansas City *Star* must undoubtedly have stimulated some characteristics which were latent in him and have introduced him to a discipline not at all uncongenial to that which he later developed into a cult. The famous *Star* style sheet—"Use short sentences. Use short first paragraphs. Use vigorous English. Be positive, not negative"— and the exacting tutelage of C. G. Wellington, the assistant city editor, could have helped to train the embryonic writer—just out of high school—to a kind of stripped, non-literary use of language where the standards of readability, accuracy, and economy would be the paramount determinants of the way scenes and events were described. Similarly, the presence of Lionel Calhoun Moise on the *Star* staff at that time, whose favorite literary advice was, "Pure objective writing is the only true form of storytelling," gives a startling anticipatory fore-shadowing of the kind of story Hemingway was to make famous. Hemingway's later employment on the two affiliated Toronto newspapers where he was given freer scope to his activities, and encouraged to write "human interest" and "humorous" stories would not have caused him to unlearn anything of value which he brought from Kansas City. What he learned would, on the other hand, give him a range of flexibility within which to experiment with prose as he could never have done on the *Star*.

There are also some less tangible areas which Hemingway's experiences as newspaper reporter and correspondent must have interlocked with the steady construction of his prose style and vision. First and obviously, he was placed in a position where he had to write on a daily earn-a-living basis. For a man who was convinced that the rules of the game required the player to learn his craft as quickly and thoroughly as possible, no better opportunity could have offered itself than the compulsory routine which journalism demanded. It is prob-ably true that these advantages quickly reach a point of diminish-ing returns; but, for the apprentice Hemingway, the almost-five years of his newspaper experience gave him a training in the manipulation of words which neither a college education nor private experimentation in writing could have afforded.

Second, and certainly equal in importance, his initiation into the newspaperman's point of view must have struck a very responsive chord in Hemingway's spirit. Confronting the hun-dreds of items of petty human behavior which stack the city desk of a major city journal every day; deliberately seeking the isolated scenes of grotesquerie, violence, and corruption which are the standard components of "the news"; and excitedly follow-ing the hospital, the police station, and the city hall "beats," Hemingway must have found strong corroboration for his al-ready developed sense of alienation. He found not only a mine of material which he would use effectively in his short stories, but also an episodic picture of the way life actually *was*.

Hemingway's newspaper experience—furthering his cynical distrust with hypocrisies of rhetoric and sharpening his critical sensitivities to men's concealed motivations—undoubtedly strengthened his "insider's" attitude. The assumption of the professional's *expertise* gained by knowing the "inside story," by interviewing such international celebrities as Clemenceau and Mussolini, would incorporate his instinctive distrust into a refusal to "be taken in" by the game; and it would harden his determination to be on the side of the manipulators rather than the manipulated. In sum, Hemingway's background as a reporter did very much the same for him that it had done earlier for Mark Twain and Theodore Dreiser: it supported him while he learned to write, it gave him the professional's arrogant contempt for the amateur and the tourist (who are always "innocents abroad"), it made him too knowing ever to be comfortable or acceptant in any situation, and it trained him in a special way of *seeing* what life was really about.

Hemingway's indebtedness to Sherwood Anderson is more difficult to assess; it is likely, in fact, that Hemingway himself overestimated the influence, which may account for the unnecessary savagery of his parody of Anderson in *The Torrents of Spring*. Hemingway told Dean Christian Gauss that he had used *Winesburg, Ohio* as his first pattern;[16] and, in spite of his disclaimers to Edmund Wilson that he had never been "inspired" by Anderson,[17] his early stories, "Up in Michigan," and "My Old Man," are very Andersonian in texture and in feeling. His friendly association with Anderson in Chicago (at a time, 1920-21, when Anderson was the only successful writer in Hemingway's acquaintance) and the older man's reputation as a revolutionary pioneer in prose would have made it certain that Hemingway read Anderson's fiction with a good deal of care. He could have found there a technique of first-person narration and a concern with the living rhythms of speech which would be very useful to him. In the loose, episodic sketches of *Winesburg, Ohio*, which at their best trail off poetically into an indefinite resonance, he could have found a pattern which might shape his Nick Adams stories into complete single units. If "My Old Man" seems to have suffered from too much conscious or unconscious derivation from a story like Anderson's "I Want to Know Why," a later story like "The Battler" seems to have learned what it needed from *Winesburg*—and gone far beyond it.

Another possible area of influence on the developing Hemingway concerns his attempts to find means to transfer emotion from the neural system to the texture of a prose narrative. We have already seen that the involuntary shock of emotion is the central element in Hemingway's aesthetic concerns. And we also know from vignettes like "On the Quai at Smyrna" or his late story, "A Man of the World" (1957), that Hemingway was willing to use almost any means to gain a legitimate *effect* on his reader. He himself would seem to have absorbed an abnormal quantity of emotional shocks, and the transference of these to the prose was to serve as both the preserver and the release of emotional intensity. Caught and frozen in the narrative, the emotion would be safe from the fritterings of time and the distortion of memory; the author, meanwhile, would have freed himself from the overcharge of his own nervous system and be able to contemplate with a greater degree of serenity the jagged contours of his own past.

Hemingway seemed to have approached this problem with a good deal of awareness and concentration, as he explains in *Death in the Afternoon*:

> I was trying to write then and I found the greatest difficulty, aside from knowing truly what you really felt, rather than what you were supposed to feel, was to put down what really happened in action; what the actual things were which produced the emotion that you experienced. . . . the real thing, the sequence of motion and fact which made the emotion and which would be as valid in a year or in ten years or, with luck, and if you stated it purely enough, always, was beyond me and I was working very hard to try to get it (2).

In his 1958 *Paris Review* interview with George Plimpton, Hemingway returns to this problem again:

> What Archie [MacLeish] was trying to remember was how I was trying to learn in Chicago in around 1920 and was searching for the unnoticed things that made emotions such as the way an outfielder tossed his glove without looking back to where it fell, the squeak of resin on canvas under a fighter's flat-soled gym shoes, the grey color of Jack Blackburn's skin when he had just come out of stir and other things I noticed as a painter sketches. You saw Blackburn's strange color and the old razor cuts and the way he spun a man before you knew his history. These were the things which moved you before you knew the story.

Hemingway's search for the "real thing"—the sensory detail which would trigger an emotional response in a prose narrative—happened to coincide with a considerable amount of literary activity dedicated to similar searches. Marcel Proust's experiments with the physical stimulations of the involuntary memory were coming to fruition. Joyce had successfully applied the "epiphany" in *Dubliners* and then with greater dexterity in *The Portrait of the Artist as a Young Man.* Thomas Mann's use of the *Leitmotif* was public currency; the followers of T. E. Hulme, the Imagists, and the unaffiliated practitioners of the New Poetry were making similar struggles with a new or refurbished use of language to create affective responses. Hemingway could have been influenced in his private search by any of these movements, or even by D. W. Griffith's pioneer applications of movie-camera close-ups.

However, Hemingway achieved the "real thing," he did develop a highly selective use of flat pictorial details which, by repetition, juxtaposition, and muted contrast with the violent situation they envelop, create a powerful tension and frequently succeed in shocking the reader into emotional awareness. It is interesting to note that T. S. Eliot published in 1919, "Hamlet and His Problems," an essay which contains the famous proposition of the "objective correlative": "The only way of expressing emotion in the form of art is by finding an 'objective correlative'; in other words, a set of objects, a situation, a chain of events which shall be the formula of that *particular* emotion; such that when the external facts, which must terminate in sensory experience, are given, the emotion is immediately evoked." It would be too much to suggest that Hemingway learned from Eliot how to capture emotion in prose, but Eliot's "objective correlative" makes an excellent definition of one of Hemingway's major techniques.

Hemingway's final influence, his relationship with Gertrude Stein, is the most difficult to evaluate because of the emotional smog cast over their mutual hostility in the 1930's.[18] Again we must try to remain within the limits of probable factual observation. Miss Stein's salon in the rue de Fleurus was one of the most exciting cultural classrooms in modern history; and Miss Stein was an appropriate lecturer. For Hemingway, between 1922 and 1924, no better place could have been found to round out his education. Erudite, keen in her appreciation of music and the visual arts, trained in psychology under Hugo Munsterberg and William James; and, above all, passionately, methodologically, opinionatedly absorbed in an attempt to revolutionize prose, Miss Stein was the ideal teacher to fill the gaps in Hemingway's education. It may be fair to say that she cleansed him of the false ontology of journalism by teaching him that reality in prose must be invented, not reported. Further, her concern with the simplification of language, of the heavy duty which the *noun* must assume, her obsessive device of repetition, and her experimentation with dialogue were all post-graduate courses which Hemingway was most eager to learn. That he might have learned them without Gertrude Stein seems beside the point. She took an interest in him, read and criticized his early manuscripts ruthlessly, and gave him practical encouragement when his submitted stories were returned to him with a regularity that must have been discouraging. It is perhaps too much the fashion today to discount Gertrude Stein as a mere eccentric and egotist; this is to forget that had she done no more than write "Melanctha," her prime place in twentieth-century fiction would be secure. And no discussion of Hemingway's development as an artist can afford to discount her unmeasurable contribution.

IV

Thus we have the "formed" Hemingway of 1924, his palette more or less complete, his characteristic approaches to the rendering of experience almost fully assembled, and his period of tutelage come to an end with the writing of his honor's thesis—"the five finger exercises"—that are the miniatures of *in our time*. It should be instructive to examine one to see what he had learned.

> They shot the six cabinet ministers at half-past six in the morning against the wall of the hospital. There were pools of water in the courtyard. There were wet dead leaves on the paving of the courtyard. It rained hard. All the shutters of the hospital were nailed shut. One of the ministers was sick with typhoid. Two soldiers carried him downstairs and out into the rain. They tried to hold him up against the wall but he sat down in a puddle of water. The other five stood very quietly against the wall. Finally the officer told the soldiers it was no good trying to make him stand up. When they fired the first volley he was sitting down in the water with his head on his knees.

The most obvious characteristic of this passage is its shocking pictorial quality. The scene exists; it is startlingly, completely *there*. And not only is it *there*, but there is a compulsive sense of slow urgency in the depiction of the scene which makes the reader feel as though he is being forced to observe this thing against his will. What he is viewing is a very "theatrical" stylized stage-set—a slowly moving *tableau* on an almost bare stage with a small number of props. There is almost no concern in the passage for the simulation of a three-dimensional illusion of reality; there are no contours, no suggestions of depth —photographic, psychological, or social.

The scene itself is as sharp and linear as an engraving, but the "flatness" is deceptive; there *is* a third dimension in the scene, which is provided by the relationship of the semi-stunned narrator to the action that is taking place before his eyes. The reader is not immediately aware of the narrator, because the reader has been insidiously placed in his viewing and reacting position. The third dimension of the picture—the quality which provides and compels the aesthetic illusion of reality, or belief— is forced out of the reader himself. In being made to *feel* the shock of the description (under the guidance of the half-concealed narrator), the reader completes the current of emotion and, as it were, validates or verifies the existential reality of the scene. This is not at all "the way it was," as early commentators on Hemingway's prose argued. It is rather the way it *is* when the successfully sensitized reader is shocked into making an involuntary emotional response to the stimuli of the prose and thereby into creating the "truth" of the description in terms of his own pulse-beat.

It is not possible for explication to demonstrate how a prose-passage like this really works; if there were tested principles of prose manipulation, then anyone could write successful prose. But explication can suggest how a particular prose passage appears to achieve its effects, and we can learn to become more aware and hence more susceptible to a writer's characteristic stylistic devices.[19] And this passage, although it appears early in Hemingway's career, is fairly representative of the kind of *effect* which was to become his hallmark. We may note, then, some of the more obvious patterns of movement which inform this scene. The sentences, with one minor exception, are all straight declarative statements, usually quite short in length. The diction is elaborately simple and there is a preponderance of monosyllabic words. Out of eleven sentences, only two ("Two soldiers. . . ." and "They tried. . . .") are definitely sequential; all the other sentences, to a greater or lesser extent, have a kind of fragmentary unconnectedness, one to the other. In other words, the logic of the scene construction is dependent neither on the stage-setting nor on the action which takes place within it, but on the fragmented *reaction* of the observer. This substitution of the logic of reaction for the logic of reported action may be one of the determinants in forcing the reader's identification with the narrator.

The simplicity of the sentence structure and of the diction is reinforced by the minimal use of adjectives and adverbs. There are no metaphors, similes, or descriptive relative clauses. In other words, the traditional techniques of achieving pictorial description have been sedulously avoided. It is important for the success of the passage that, while the scene must have intensive clarity, it must not be too solidly rooted in a situation of objective reality; it must be free to detach itself from its spatial-temporal background and come to objectification in someone's inner consciousness. Further, the careful use of repetition—repeated constructions, words, and near rhymes—which allies itself with the muted rhythmical quality of the passage, reinforces the echo of the narrator's presence. It can be only his voice which is talking, and the unvarying monotone of that voice sets the audial frame for the emotional response.

Finally, the selection of details is patently controlled by Hemingway's attempts to select just those details which will evoke and control the desired emotional response. Here the objective correlative of the emotion is defined by the rain, the pools of water in the courtyard, the wet dead leaves, and the final sordid puddle of water in which the sixth cabinet minister sits down to receive his death. This image-pattern, which moves from the pools on the ground to the sky ("It rained hard") and then back down to the ground again, is paralleled by the descent of the sixth minister ("Two soldiers carried him downstairs. . . .) who ("his head on his knees") completes the vignette in a closed, sodden collapse. The pattern of images is actually quite traditional; and, with the insertion of the "wet dead leaves," it is almost sentimental. The saving detail, which testifies to Hemingway's success in observing "the unnoticed things that made emotions," is the line: "All the shutters of the hospital were nailed shut." This, it seems to me, is the "gooseflesh" line in the sketch—the muted detail which operates on an almost subliminal level to release emotional resonance. It is stark, final ("shutters" are "shut") and claustrophobic. The hospital—the place of restoration to health, the monument to normality—is sordidly degraded. We could even reluctantly suggest a hint of crucifixion imagery in "nailed" and a suggestion that, in the shuttering up of the hospital windows, the eyes of health and normality have been stricken with outraged blindness. The fact is that this line *works*; how or why it works we cannot really know, but it seems to have something to do with "the real thing" that Hemingway sought.

V

Stylistic analysis which attempts to be interpretative is always to some degree subjective and, whether admittedly or not, operative under *a priori* commitments. Yet it is interesting to project from such an analysis what kinds of attitudes, effects, limitations, and strengths we can expect in Hemingway's prose. Some of these have been discussed earlier and others implied; we will now attempt to sum up the implicit aesthetic, or—to return to an earlier metaphor—to describe more accurately the nature and design of Hemingway's weapon against the world.

On the basis of what we have seen, Robert Penn Warren's description of Hemingway is pithily accurate: "[he is essentially a] lyric rather than a dramatic writer, and for the lyric writer virtue depends upon the intensity with which the personal vision is rendered rather than upon the creation of a variety of characters whose visions are in conflict among themselves."[20] While it is not exactly fair to make the early Hemingway vignette bear the burden of so much interpretation, we can see from it that the only character of real interest in it is the narrating voice. The five docile ministers, the sick one, the soldiers, and the officer have as much but no more importance than the puddles and pools, the leaves, the hospital shutters, and the rain. They are all—animate or inanimate—counters which really don't count in the game, except as they mirror or enflesh the state of mind of the narrator.

And because of this need for a lyrical outlet for his personal vision, we will find that the typical Hemingway fiction will be of two closely related types. Either there will be an actual or an implied first person-narrator (the Nick Adams stories, *The Sun Also Rises, A Farewell to Arms*), or there will be seemingly objective third-person narrated fictions in which the reader will be coerced into the position of the reacting, unspeaking "voice" (*The Old Man and the Sea*). We will investigate these kinds of fictional structures in detail later, but we may point out here that Hemingway is likely to run into trouble whenever he departs from this format. Because the Hemingway fiction generates its form and its strength from its capacity to deliver an emotional shock, or "punch," the creation of a surrogate reacting character (or "punchingbag") will be mandatory; and the kinds of characters and situations which he can invent will be dependent on this structural determinant.

Further, because Hemingway is attempting to capture emotional intensity *in time* and to make it *timeless*—safe from the onslaughts of distorting memory and the erosion of the temporal —we can expect his fictions to take place in a world which is, as Carlos Baker suggests, "screened . . . at both ends."[21] His fictional worlds may have illusory geographical settings; they may be located on a map or in history, but this seeming objective authenticity will be a functional *divertissement* to engage the reader in the emotional context of the *personal* and not the *public* vision. Hence the fictional worlds will tend to be enclosed and removed, existentially rootless as surreal landscapes in which the reader and the narrator (overt or covert) may share in their inward realities. Hemingway's work has frequently been unjustly criticized on this point by critics determined to apply the measurements of objective realism (or naturalism) to materials that are simply incompatible with those measurements. The preceding miniature is a fair demonstration of this. It is devoid of social-historical reality—and purposely so. It may or may not have been based on an actual occurrence, and it may even make an indirect contribution to historical understanding. But, as it stands on the page, it is primarily a nightmare emotion, recollected or invented within an artifice of simulated shock.

In varying degrees this "out-of-space out-of-timeliness" holds true for almost all of Hemingway's fiction. Hemingway confused the issue by declaring in *Green Hills of Africa* that "where we go, if we are any good, there you can go as we have been." It would be fruitless and unjust to Hemingway to invoke this as a literal test. His cherished landscapes merge together; his rivers are all pretty similar whether they flow in Spain, Italy, the Black Forest, or Upper Michigan. Mountains and meadows, villages and large cities—they are all individually believable within their own artistic-emotional contexts; but, taken out of them, they are indistinguishable, except by the place-names, the slight variations in folk-idiom, and the distinctive peculiarities of locale which even Hemingway couldn't disguise. But in a more important and valuable sense, Hemingway's declaration is quite true, especially in those descriptions where he finds the objective correlative for his reactions to places. Hemingway's exceptional forte was not to describe what he saw, but to describe himself *seeing*, to convey the complex of feeling which was invoked in him or in an invented character when that character was placed in an appropriate situation of tension.[22] This *there* he could and did render with wonderful precision and complex tonality; and to this *there* countless readers have been able to follow him.

The thrust of this central characteristic of Hemingway's aesthetic is to move his stories away from fiction toward fable—away from a concern with the concrete and the particular toward the universal and the symbolic. Hemingway's "lyric" need to project his personal vision of the world suggests that the personal vision may become so overriding as to supplant the "objective" world when they come in conflict with one another. Saul Bellow brilliantly perceived this danger in his review of *The Old Man and the Sea*, but the tendency is also present in Hemingway's earliest fictions: "He tends to speak for Nature itself. Should Nature and Hemingway become identical one or the other will have won too total a victory."[23] It was Nature that ultimately won the victory, but the conflict that he carried on against Nature—and it was a "total" conflict—provided him and us with the products of his art. "Let those who want to save the world if you can get to see it clear and as a whole. Then any part you make will represent the whole if it's made truly." These words, which have such an Emersonian ring, become potentially dangerous when the only test of "clearness" and "wholeness" is involuntary emotional responses. When truth, goodness, and beauty—in traditional romantic fashion—are based on the neural shudder that raises the gooseflesh on the skin, and when the skin belongs to a man hypersensitively aware of his own isolation and excessively prone to lash out from behind his many masks before he himself suffers a hurt—then the literary critic may be excused his romantic speculation that perhaps Herman Melville invented Hemingway over a century ago.

The aesthetic directions of an Ahabian vision are at least not speculative. We can expect that Hemingway's fictions will move from dramatic concerns to the enactment of myth; that his focus will concern itself less and less with men, and more and more with Man; and that Man will tend to be cast in the image of its undivine creator. We can also expect that Death, the universal antagonist of the cosmos, will have to be neutralized in some fashion by an artist who has chosen the course of antagonism against a hostile universe; and we realize that this neutralization may require a tacit truce or even a working alliance between the artist and Death.

Concerning his ideal artist-bullfighter Hemingway wrote in *Death in the Afternoon*: "A great killer must love to kill; unless he feels that it is the best thing he can do, unless he is conscious of its dignity and feels that it is its own reward, he will be incapable of the abnegation that is necessary in real killing. The truly great killer must have a sense of honor and a sense of glory far beyond that of the ordinary bullfighter. In other words he must be a simpler man." (232).

And D. H. Lawrence, summing up what seemed to him the very essence of the American spirit and the true business of the American myth, wrote:

> The essential American soul is hard, isolate, stoic, and a killer. It has never yet melted.
> Of course the soul often breaks down into disintegration. . . .
> What true myth concerns itself with is not the disintegration product. True myth concerns itself centrally with the onward adventure of the integral soul. And this, for America, is Deerslayer. A man who turns his back on white society. A man who keeps his moral integrity hard and intact. An isolate, almost selfless, stoic enduring man, who lives by death, by killing, but who is pure white.

An examination of Hemingway's aesthetic ends inevitably in a contemplation of the Lawrentian version of the true American myth. It remains to see whether we are dealing with "the disintegration product" or the work of "a simpler man" whose soul "has never yet melted."

CHAPTER 3

Of Tyros and Tutors

I

HEMINGWAY'S VISION, based on his need to relate his isolate self to all that was *not*-self, was, as we have seen, an intensely lyrical vision; yet he is not a poet but a writer of fiction.[1] When he says in *Green Hills of Africa* that he is striving to create a prose "much more difficult than poetry," he is not indulging in casual hyperbole. He is actually stating quite accurately the dilemma that his aesthetic demands and his storytelling talents forced upon him. Given his insatiable drive to make his identity metaphysically secure through attaching it to the *things* of the universe by, as it were, emotional adhesion, we might have expected him to write a prose equivalent to "Song of Myself" or *The Waste Land*. In these poems—as in the last chapter of *Death in the Afternoon*, in Harry's remembrances of things past in "The Snows of Kilimanjaro," or in his preface to Vittorini's *In Sicily*—the principles of aesthetic and metaphysical structure fuse in the device of the evocative catalogue. The metaphysical selves of the artists (their identities, in the full sense) are created and realized in their recollected moments of sincere emotional response; these, in turn, are recreated artistically as the fragments they have shored against their ruins.[2]

But Hemingway differed from both Whitman and Eliot in very significant ways. Unlike Whitman, he prized the adamant separateness of his isolate self, as we can see in his choice to be an administrator of death rather than a wooer of it. He fiercely resisted any potential loss of self, even a loss which might have given him the incalculable gain of transcendent mergence. There is in Hemingway a curious deficiency in the capacity to love which becomes manifest when we compare him to Whitman; the latter could write love poems to "sweet soothing death" and become whole in the spirit of total communion; Hemingway's book on bullfighting is a kind of love song to killing which insures him the role of eternal opposition. "The kelson of the creation is love," sang Whitman. But for Hemingway the kelson had cracked right down the middle, and the creation had become a form of combat in which "the conditions are that the winner shall take nothing."

And, unlike Eliot—whose revulsion at the world was matched by his revulsion at his own sensory responses—Hemingway could not deny the fundamental *joie de vivre* of experiencing physical action, of delighting in the increased awareness of life and self which the operation of his five senses so abundantly offered him. Eliot could try to enter the realms of all-acceptant love by a firm denial of the self that he found so distasteful; once there, his "vision of the street" could become softened into a prayerful meditation where "the fire and the rose are one." But Hemingway's deficiencies in his powers to love are matched by his incapacity to really hate. He can be contemptuous; he can be shocked and outraged; he can be arrogantly superior. But lacking a sense of real security in the universe, he lacked also the necessary bases of self-righteousness and self-unity, the sources of hatred. And thus again, for precisely the reverse reasons as with Whitman, Hemingway was forced into the role of eternal opposition in total conflict with everything that was Other.

This introductory discussion is pertinent if it helps us to realize why Hemingway had no choice except to *dramatize* his lyric vision. The uncompromising split that he felt between himself and the universe could be made to yield an objective correlative of his emotions only through the tensions of the dialectic form. Action and reaction, force and shock, challenge and response—these are the relentless antagonists which will engage in dubious battle throughout Hemingway's fiction; the battlefield, the locus of contact and the point of arrest, is the *willed awareness* of the human spirit, Hemingway's spirit, recording with precision the attacks and counterattacks, the retreats, the acts of bravery and cowardice, the casualties and the irreparable damages. In order to examine the dramatic tension which provides the action of his fictions, we will have to examine in some detail the famous Hemingway "Hero" and Hemingway's "Code" within the general frame of reference which we have been developing.[3]

II

There are, as criticism has come slowly to recognize, not one but two Hemingway heroes; or, to use Philip Young's designations, the "Nick-Adams-hero" and the "code-hero." The generic Nick Adams character, who lives through the course of Hemingway's fiction, appears first as the shocked invisible "voice" of the miniatures of *in our time*; he grows up through Hemingway's three volumes of short stories and at least four of his novels, sometimes changing his name to Jake Barnes, Frederick Henry, Mr. Frazer, Macomber, Harry, Robert Jordan, Richard Cantwell; and he makes his final appearances (appropriately un-named as when he first entered the fictional stage) in Hemingway's last two published stories in 1957. The code-hero also figures in Hemingway's earliest fiction. He dies of a *cogida* as Maera in *in our time*, and he is resurrected in a considerable variety of shapes, forms, and accents (usually non-American) through the bulk of Hemingway's creative output. His manifestations would include the Belmonte of *The Sun Also Rises*; Manuel in "The Undefeated"; the Major of "In Another Country"; Harry Morgan, Wilson of "The Short Happy Life of Francis Macomber"; Cayetano Ruiz, of "The Gambler, the Nun, and the Radio"; El Sordo, and Santiago.

For convenience sake I will refer to the Nick Adams hero as the *tyro* and to the "code-hero" as the *tutor;* for it is basically an educational relationship, albeit a very one-sided one, which binds them together. The tyro, faced with the overwhelming confusion and hurt (*nada*) inherent in an attempt to live an active sensual life, admires the deliberate self-containment of the tutor (a much "simpler man") who is seemingly not beset with inner uncertainties. Accordingly, the tyro tries to model his behavior on the pattern he discerns. However, the tyro is *not* a simple man; being in fact a very near projection of Hemingway himself, he is never able to attain the state of serene unself-consciousness—what James once called nastily "the deep intellectual repose"—that seems to come naturally to the tutor. What he can learn, however, is the *appearance* of that self-containment. He can laboriously train himself in the conventions of the appearance which is "the code"; and he can so severely practice those external restraints as to be provided with a pragmatic defense against the horrors that never cease to assault him.

It may be salutary to digress slightly to what we can call "The Education of Nick Adams" because there is some inevitable confusion surrounding it. In one sense the education is thoroughly abortive; Nick at the end of his multi-chequered career is as terrified and lost as he was, for example, in his encounter with the stark, machined horror of the Chicago gangsters in "The Killers." In the following quotation is the tyro, aged somewhere in his mid-fifties, trying to cope with the loss of his eyesight ("Get a Seeing-Eyed Dog"): "Because I am not doing too well at this. That I can promise you. But what else can you do? Nothing, he thought. There's nothing you can do. But maybe, as you go along, you will get good at it." The tyro, with his unfair inheritance from Hemingway of a particularly fecund and hyperactive imagination of disaster, has lost nothing of his capacities to be afraid—in spite of his long indoctrination in the craft of courage. In fact, he has rather increased his capacities, for his accumulated experience of horror has taught him many more things of which to be afraid. Measured pragmatically, however—and the defense never pretends to be more than a pragmatic one—Nick *does* survive for an astonishingly long time. He does, as Hemingway puts it, get pretty good at it as he goes along.

If we sketch briefly Nick's biography, we will be able to judge somewhat better the values of his education and to note also the varying ways that Hemingway employed him as shock absorber and seismographer of emotional stress. Nick is born, roughly at the turn of the twentieth century, somewhere in the Midwest. His father, a physician, is fond of hunting and shooting, and is concerned to teach Nick the proper ways of handling a rod and a gun. Dr. Adams has incredibly sharp eyesight and is a better wing-shot than Nick will ever be. He is also intimidated by his wife—a suspiciously indistinct character who is a blur of polite nagging and vague religious sentiments—and, on one occasion, Nick is shocked to see his father back down from a fight. The pattern of cowardice and intimidation, never actually explained, comes to a disgusting (to Nick) finale when his father commits suicide in the 1920's with Nick's grandfather's gun. The grandfather becomes elected as Nick's spiritual father—a tutorial hero because of his reputed bravery during the Civil War.

As a boy, Nick's adventures are an extreme distillation of the excitements, perplexities, and terrors that are classically supposed to accompany adolescence. He witnesses a lynching in Ohio, a Caesarean delivery by jack-knife and a razor suicide in an Indian camp; he has a very satisfactory initiation into sex with an Ojibway Indian girl whom he later discovers to be promiscuous. He also undergoes a puppylove affair with a "nice" girl, which he is tremulously strong enough to break off. Unexplainedly "on the road," he comes into contact with sentimental whores, sinister homosexuals, and a vaudeville team of professional assassins. His characteristic response to the situations in which he finds himself is open-eyed shock; he registers the events as though he were a slow-motion camera, but rarely if ever does he actively participate in these events. He never really gets into a fight; he does not argue; he does not retreat to protect his sensibilities. Like the camera, he has a curious masochistic quality of total acceptance and receptivity. At about this point we begin to suspect that the adventures of Nick Adams are approximately as realistic as "The Adventures of Tom Swift," although any individual episode in the serial is gratifyingly convincing. We begin to suspect that Hemingway's tyro figure is a projection into the nightmare possibilities of confusion, pain, and immolation; that his adventures are mythic fantasies, guided by the rhythms of intense fear and alienation. That, in short, Nick Adams is a sacrificial victim, bound time and time again to the slaughtering-table to be *almost* slaughtered in order that his creator and readers may be free of fear.

The pattern continues and proliferates when Nick joins the Italian Army fighting the Austrians in northeastern Italy. He is blown up at Fossalta di Piave, where he feels his soul go out of his body, go off, and then return. For a long time after this he has to leave the light burning at night to keep his soul in place. His convalescence at the hospital in Milan is aided and abetted by a love-affair with a British nurse, but he is finally returned to the Austrian front as a morale advertisement—in spite of the fact that he is in a severe state of combat trauma. He returns briefly to the United States to go fishing, and then re-embarks for Europe where he remains except for sporadic visits to hunt in Wyoming and to recuperate from an accident in a Montana hospital. Somewhere along the line he has become by profession a writer—more often a newspaperman—and he has also married. There is surprisingly little information about his domestic life, other than that he is afraid his approaching fatherhood will put a restraint on his athletic diversions. Much later we discover that he has been married and divorced three times; but, in general, the nightmare terrors of banal marital existence are avoided in the episodes of his adventures.

We catch glimpses of his life in the 1920's—skiing in Switzerland, riding his bicycle through Paris streets, developing an air of *expertise* on the running of the bulls in Spain and the empty carousing of the American bohemians throughout Europe. Details of isolated horror in World War I crop up in his memories from time to time, and the action of the Greeks in breaking the legs of their baggage animals and dumping them in the harbor at Smyrna (Izmir) becomes a kind of climactic *Leitmotif* in the aria of his remembered terrors. But meanwhile there has been a gradual hardening of his powers to resist the shocks which he seems desperately impelled to pursue. He slowly edges away from the margins of nervous collapse as a war convalescent who has seen too many helmets full of brains. Painfully during the 1920's, he masters his physical responses and rather proudly subjects himself to situations of violence and disgust as though (like the red-headed Vet in *To Have and Have Not*) these occasions give him an opportunity to prove that he can not only absorb punishment but also take a perverted pleasure in it.

The 1930's extend his experience to the fishing waters between Cuba and Key West, safaris to Africa, and the Loyalist front in the Spanish War. Nick, who has become increasingly resistant to shock, reacts now more as a clinical observer than as an outraged participant. In fact, there is evidence that he even manipulates events consciously to increase a stress-situation, as when—through "the always dirty desire to see how people act under an emotional conflict, that makes writers such attractive friends"[4]—he triggers off a rather unpleasant series of consequences which leads to the execution of one man and the guilty shame of another. His exposures to the cynicism of political chicanery in the command levels of the Spanish War are followed by disgust with the military stupidities and vanities of the higher echelons which control the operations of World War II. The threat of old age and physical debility appears in his collection of terrors in the late 1930's, becomes a more dense spectre in the 1940's, and assumes haunting proportions in the 1950's in his recurrent fear of blindness. The question of suicide, introduced in the early 1930's, remains a foreboding undercurrent in his ethical reflections through the 1940's and 1950's; and it is probably significant that his first aggressive denunciation of the act becomes reluctantly mollified. And, finally, a marginal interest in Catholic attitudes toward life and death, which appears in the 1920's, maintains its steady flow throughout his career, without seeming to engage his deeper levels of concern.

Such is Nick Adams, surely *not*, as one critic explains, "[the story of a man's life which] differs in no essential way from that of almost any middleclass American male who started life at the beginning of the present century or even with the generation of 1920."[5] There is very little that is realistically representative in the career of Nicholas Adams, nor, I would submit, is there meant to be. In a sense—which his name suggests—he is a released devil of our innocence, an enfleshment of our conscious and unconscious fears dispatched to do battle with the frightening possibilities that an always uncertain future holds over our heads. He is the whipping-boy of our fearful awareness, the pragmatic probability extrapolated into a possible tomorrow to serve as a propitiary buffer against the evils which tomorrow may or may not bring. He suffers our accidents and defeats before they happen to us. Like Tiresias, he is doomed to foresuffer them all—to witness the infidelities and deaths of our loved ones; to enact our cowardices and indecisions; to struggle against the internal and external diseases which inexorably pursue us; in short, to die the innumerable times we project our deaths in our imaginations. But for all this he is a far from impotent counter in the game in which the winner takes nothing. Hemingway plays him as the sacrificial card in his hand which will finesse the ruthless king; he is the defeated victim, but in experiencing his defeat, Hemingway (and we) can ring ourselves in invisible armor so that we will be undefeated if and when the catastrophes of our imagination do actually occur. On this level, then, the Nick Adams projection is a vital defensive weapon in Hemingway's combat with the universe.

III

The tutor, on the other hand, is a much less complicated figure than the tyro; but he is certainly no more realistic. If the tyro is in general a projection of the possibilities of an inadequate response to "the terrible ambiguities of an immediate experience" (Jung's phrase), the tutor is the embodied wish-fulfillment of a successful response. He is "a tough boy," which Colonel Cantwell defines as "a man who will make his play and then back it up. Or just a man who backs his play." The seemingly innocuous amendment to the definition underlines one distinction between the tutor and the tyro. The fully developed tyro is "the man who will make his play and then back it up." The tutor is "just a man who backs his play." The difference, so deceptively small, encompasses the whole range of man's conscious awareness of himself while engaged in action; it includes his capacities not only to reflect and to imagine but also to be aware of reflecting and imagining. This human burden the tyro must always carry, but from it the tutor is free; this, indeed, is what makes the tutor "a simpler man." He is so simple, in fact, that he is closer to brute animality than to "humanness."[6] For example, we cite Manuel of "The Undefeated" as he is facing the bull which will not charge:

> He thought in bull-fight terms. Sometimes he had a thought and the particular piece of slang would not come into his mind and he could not realize the thought. His instincts and his knowledge worked automatically, and his brain worked slowly and in words. He knew all about bulls. He did not have to think about them. He just did the right thing. His eyes noted things and his body performed the necessary measures without thought. If he thought about it, he would be gone.

Thought and action (or reaction) are simultaneous for Manuel; he is "just a man who backs his play," and hence his responses will be inevitably adequate to the challenge that he is trained to accept. The tyro, as we see often in Hemingway's works, must try to stop himself from thinking. There is an inevitable hiatus between challenge and response, action and reaction; it is here, in Hemingway's diagnosis, that man's greatest danger takes place. The broken circuit, the incomplete synapse, the failure of the nerve: all these phrases designate that emotional paralysis, or shock, which Hemingway had every reason to fear, and which on a collective basis may very well be the major disease of twentieth-century man. Thus the trained tyro is "the man who will make his play and then back it up"; unable to become a fully responsive mechanism of instincts, he can try to condition himself to force the right responses under stress.

The tutor takes a surprisingly large variety of forms in Hemingway's fiction, but, in each of his manifestations, he is always "the professional." With two significant exceptions, his activities are confined to areas where he can perform within the predictabilities of his training—fighting bulls, bootlegging whiskey and Chinamen, facing lion charges, and landing large fish. The exceptional stories recount, in part, the adventures of tutors who encounter challenges beyond the jurisdiction of their professional preparations; these are in "Fifty Grand" and "In Another Country."

"Fifty Grand," one of Hemingway's most humorous stories, recalls Ring Lardner's "Champion" in tone and situation. The tutor is Jack Brennan—loutish, parsimonious, over-aged welterweight champion of the world. Believing honestly that he will lose his title to the challenger, Walcott, he bets fifty thousand dollars against himself. He does not know, however, that a gambling syndicate has arranged for Walcott to throw the fight. In the eleventh round, when it is obvious that Brennan (who has been making an honest fight thus far) will eventually lose on points, Walcott deliberately fouls him and seriously hurts him in the process. The situation is supremely comical: if Brennan abides by the rules of boxing, as well as by the imperatives of his creature instincts (he is in much pain) and his professional conditioning, he will retain his championship and lose fifty thousand dollars. Instead, he waves off the referee and brutally fouls Walcott twice, losing the fight on a foul and winning his bet. And he remarks toward the end of the story, "It's funny how fast you can think when it means that much money."

One critic has dubbed this to be a story of the "honor-and-courage-among-thieves" variety, finding Brennan a satisfactory code hero in the peculiar milieu of his operations.[7] This interpretation, however, misses the humor and the point of the story. What we have is an exposure in veniality to the non-committed first-person narrator (the tyro), and an indication that professionals (tutors) can be trusted only within their special areas of mastery. Brennan breaks the code in betting against himself, and when he is challenged by the foul, he is thrown like the rest of us into a decision-making problem where his training is useless. His exercise of "fast" thinking under stress transforms him from a fully responsive mechanism of instincts into an instinctive machine of avarice.

"In Another Country," which is surely one of Hemingway's masterpieces in the short story form, also takes a professional into a challenge situation for which he has not been prepared, but with very different results from the satiric "Fifty Grand." The Major of the story is Hemingway's most attractive tutor figure, and he is also the most intelligent and sensitive. A professional soldier, and before the war a champion fencer, he is undergoing mechanical therapy for a wound which has left his fencing hand shrunken to baby size. Disabling wounds and death are foreseeable eventualities for professional soldiers, and the Major accepts his lot with equanimity. Out of a sense of duty he reports to the hospital every afternoon to be treated by the therapeutic machines (designed to rehabilitate industrial accidents), even though he does not believe in their efficacy. When he engages the tyro (the first-person narrator) in conversation, he insists with characteristic professionalism that the boy speak Italian grammatically. As Hemingway presents him, the Major is a figure of considerable dignity and somewhat stuffy rectitude who "did not believe in bravery," presumably because, like Santiago, he chooses precision and exactness over the uncontrollable results of impulse action.

But one afternoon he comes to the hospital in a very irritable mood and provokes the tyro into a rude argument over marriage in which he declaims angrily that a man must not marry. "If he is to lose everything, he should not place himself in a position to lose that. He should not place himself in a position to lose. He should find things he cannot lose." He makes a telephone call and returns to the room where the tyro is sitting.

> He was wearing his cape and had his cap on, and he came directly toward my machine and put his arm on my shoulder.
>
> "I am so sorry," he said, and patted me on the shoulder with his good hand. "I would not be rude. My wife has just died. You must forgive me."
>
> "Oh—" I said, feeling sick for him. "I am *so* sorry."
>
> He stood there biting his lower lip. "It is very difficult," he said. "I cannot resign myself."
>
> He looked straight past me and out through the window. Then he began to cry. "I am utterly unable to resign myself," he said and choked. And then crying, his head up looking at nothing, carrying himself straight and soldierly, with tears on both his cheeks and biting his lips, he walked past the machines and out the door.

One final paragraph concludes the story, in which we are told that the Major returns for his regular treatments three days later with mourning crepe on his uniform sleeve. The doctors had placed photographs of wounds before and after treatment in front of his machine. "The photographs did not make much difference to the major because he only looked out of the window."

This is the one certain case in Hemingway's work where the tutor rises far beyond the artificial boundaries that restrict his need to make decisions. As we have seen, the code of professionalism with its severe conditioning in special pragmatic skills and attitudes is designed to minimize the multiplicity of possibilities existing in any challenge situation. Or, to express it more simply, the professional attitude creates an arbitrary chart of the future—like a contour map of preselected terrain—in which only a few items are considered significant and the rest are ignored. The rationale for the adoption of such a code is suggested in the Major's passionate cry: "[Man] should not place himself in a position to lose. He should find things he cannot lose." He will eventually lose everything when he loses himself, but along the way he will be able to control his losses and also the sequence of "holding attacks" through which he wages his battles.

If such a life code were adhered to strictly, a man would have to be either "the dumb ox" (the "simpler man") of so much Hemingway criticism or an unbelievable monster of machined egotism living, as it were, in an almost impregnable pillbox with no exits or entrances. The Major of this story is neither; his adoption of a code of life does not preclude his exposure to the risks of the incalculable in spite of his angry cry of outrage. Because he is human, he has loved; and, to continue the military metaphor, he has wittingly exposed his flanks to undefendable attack. His commitment to love and his shock at his wife's death have placed him "in another country" than the one he has prepared to defend. That other country is nothing less than the human condition itself, for the human will is always vulnerable to ruthless destruction. And Hemingway's ultimate test of human performance is the degree of stripped courage and dignity which man can discover in himself in his moments of absolute despair. It would have been quite simple for the Major to have died well; his challenge is far greater than his own death (a challenge which Hemingway has typically considered a relatively easy one to face). The Major, in losing his wife, suffers a death of himself accompanied by the absurdity of his own continued life. It is meaninglessness—*nada*—that confronts the Major in full assault.

And like Jesus in "Today is Friday," the Major is "good in there." He is badly broken, but not destroyed. He refuses to resign himself to the chaos of un-meaning, but he refuses also to deny the actuality of his fearsome defeat. He holds tight to the superficial conventions of his training—the empty forms of innate courtesy and soldierly duty—and sits within them to begin the laborious process of making the broken places within himself strong again. His response can be characterized as neither acceptance nor denial; he is neither victim nor rebel. The least and the best that can be said of him is that he survives with dignity, and it is possible that he may be considered Hemingway's most eloquent portrait of ideal heroism— unquixotic, unathletic, profoundly humanistic.

The characteristic of *dignity*, so important to Hemingway as to have furnished him with one of the major themes in his fiction, is relevant to our discussion at this point. The peculiar problems of twentieth-century life have made the depictions of human dignity almost anomalous in modern literature. Our characteristic heroes have been "anti-heroes" or non-heroes, aggressive doomed men in revolt or essentially pathetic dupes at the mercy of non-malicious and implacable victimization. Dignity in either situation is difficult to ascribe to such heroes who tend by choice to divest themselves of the traditional values of rational intelligence and moral integrity on which dignity has always rested. The great majority of modern heroes in literature are purposely grotesque—picaresque saints, rebels, victims, and underground men of all shapes and colors. Their individual value as artistic achievements and embodiments of viable life attitudes is undeniable, but *dignity* is a quality largely beyond their grasp.[8] Hemingway's attempt to retain the ideal of dignity without falsifying the ignobility of the modern human condition (that impulse in his work which leads many commentators to associate his beliefs with those of classical Stoicism) is one of his signal triumphs as a modern writer. And it is generally through his characterizations of the tutor figure that this quality of dignity is manifested.

Besides the Major we can find it in Manuel ("The Undefeated"), in Anselmo of *For Whom the Bell Tolls,* in the old men of "A Clean Well-Lighted Place" and of "Old Man at the Bridge," and finally in Santiago. It is probably significant that all of these examples are old, or at least older men. Dignity certainly does not come automatically with age in Hemingway's fiction, but it is usually denied to youth with its passions and penchant for illusions.[9] A minimal degree of native intelligence is a basic requirement; basic also are the qualities of real humility and self-abnegation. Thus characters like Harry Morgan, Cayetano Ruiz, Wilson, or El Sordo—all in some fashion tutor figures and models of a kind of excellence—are on the lower levels of Hemingway's portraits of heroism. This point should be remembered since too many evaluations of Hemingway's life code are based on the mistaken assumption that Hemingway's code heroes can be lumped together in an indiscriminate stereotype of brute primitivism and animal virtues.

One other point should be made concerning the tutor figure. We have noted that the great majority of them are non-American (Spanish bullfighters, Mexican gamblers, British white hunters, etc.), and that the ones of greatest excellence, of *dignity,* are all non-Americans and men of mature or advanced age. We also noted earlier that Hemingway's nubile heroines are likewise non-Americans and that, if they do not grow progressively younger as Hemingway writes over a period of some thirty years, they do not noticeably age either. His heroines would seem to be so many variations on his archetype, the Ojibway Trudy (the chippie from the old block), and these two examples of repetitive characterization should offer some evidence for legitimate speculation. Just as we have seen that the Nick Adams projection can be understood as a compulsive fantasy figure closely related to one aspect of Hemingway's self-image, so these two other consistent figurations are comparable fantasy projections. It takes no great amount of Freudian sophistication to recognize that the tutor figure is an obvious father image. Purified of the weaknesses that shame Nick in his real hunting-and-fishing father, the substitute retains the capacity to "doctor" or heal by emulation. All the tutor fathers are childless (Harry Morgan has a brood of daughters); and, in suffering the seachange of denationalization and conversion to Catholicism, they are moved by Hemingway into another country where they can be loved and respected by their tyro sons without reservation. The heroines, similarly, would seem to be purified mother figures; at once completely satisfying and undemanding, they are handy oceanic reservoirs of temporary regression and security. The incest motif that obtrudes from *Across the River and Into the Trees* can thus be seen as a rather consistent modulation on the erotic concerns in Hemingway's fiction.

The relationship between Colonel Cantwell and Renata affords us an opportunity of investigating the Hemingway heroine somewhat more closely.[10] Renata is "almost nineteen," the age at which Nick Adams and Cantwell suffered the great wound at Fossalta di Piave. Cantwell refers to Renata and to her symbolic portrait as "boy" and "daughter," suggesting that Hemingway is employing the device of "symbolic doubling" (Carlos Baker's term) to make Renata not only the mother image (the daughter inversion is a standard Freudian trick) of Cantwell, but also his alter ego or *anima*—that is, himself some thirty years earlier. The temporary gift of the two emeralds which Renata presents to Cantwell is clearly symbolic of Cantwell's youthful virility; and Renata's name ("the reborn") would seem to make this reading decisive.

Extending this interpretation to Hemingway's other typical heroines, Catherin Barkley and Maria, we find that the double function of each is likewise present but is less obvious. Each becomes absolutely identified with her lover: "There isn't any me. I'm you." And in the physical act of union—symbolically appropriate in a womb-like sleeping bag or under a blanket in a Venetian gondola—the tyro figure makes a complete regression to a pre-natal state of oneness with himself and mother. Finally we may note that in *The Old Man and the Sea*, Hemingway's last published major work, the impulse to regression is complete. The tyro has split into the young boy, Manolo, and the hero, Santiago, while the Hemingway heroine (the mother and *anima*) has assumed its primordial symbolic shape as *la mar*, the eternal, feminine sea.

IV

I am neither interested, nor qualified, to conduct a fully developed psychoanalytic study of Hemingway's fiction, which, to my knowledge has never been made; but an elementary analytic reading can illuminate some of the conditions of Hemingway's art. The point that is worth grasping here, as we have been insisting, is that Hemingway's aesthetic concerns are not with the depiction of objective reality, but with the fantasy-projections of his inner consciousness. The mirror of his art is held up to his own nature, not Nature; and, if he succeeded in casting a definition of the human condition which has been useful to twentieth-century readers, it is because his own human condition, painfully and honestly transmuted into evocative prose in a lifetime of disciplined writing, was in some way deeply representative of the condition of humanity. We can never really know how aware he was of the direction that his art took. We do know that it was compulsively intent on recording those emotional shocks that gave him a feeling of immortality. We know also that he wrote in order that he could live, and when he could no longer "get rid of it" (the disintegrating shocks) through writing them out, he ceased to live. The pattern of his work is consistently rooted in a dramatization of the traumatic births of his tortured psyche, relentlessly struggling to rid itself of its horrors. An examination of one of the problems recurrent in Hemingway criticism may be persuasive in showing that the real pain in Hemingway's fiction is residual in his personality, and that he may very well be talking about his own theory of writing when he asks through Richard Gordon (the writer in *To Have and Have Not*): "Why must all the operations in life be performed without an anaesthetic?"

The inconsistency of Hemingway's socio-political beliefs has been, since the middle 1930's, a stumbling-block or source of embarrassment to Hemingway's critics, both the friendly and the hostile. A writer, like everyone else, has every right to change his mind on cardinal principles of belief; but a writer, especially a great writer, is under obligation to leave a trail of evidence behind him in his shifts of opinion, so that his devious course can be followed. In the miniatures of *in our time* (1924), Hemingway proclaimed the "separate peace"; and he officially ratified it in the famous baptismal plunge into the Tagliamento River in *A Farewell to Arms* (1929):

> You had lost your cars and your men as a floorwalker loses the stock of his department in a fire. There was, however, no insur-/ ance. You were out of it now. You had no more obligation. . . .
>   Anger was washed away in the river along with any obligation. . . . I had taken off the stars, but that was for convenience. It was no point of honor. I was not against them. I was through. I wished them all the luck. . . . But it was not my show anymore (248).

Frederick Henry's political "lone-wolfism" and his disseverance from any body of authority is strictly held to through *Death in the Afternoon* (1932) and *Green Hills of Africa* (1935); if anything, his determination to be uninvolved is more pronounced. And yet, in an amazingly sudden turnabout, Hemingway renounces the separate peace with Harry Morgan's dramatically unmotivated dying speech in *To Have and Have Not* (1937): "No matter how a man alone ain't got no bloody . . . chance." And the shift is spelled out as clearly as possible with Robert Jordan's voluntary enlistment against Fascism in *For Whom the Bell Tolls* (1940).

The nub of the literary critical confusion in Hemingway's political shifts is that Robert Jordan submits to Communist discipline for reasons which are precisely antithetical to those that impel Frederick Henry's desertion. Henry stands for the concrete immediacy of experience and is "embarrassed by the words sacred, glorious, and sacrifice and the expression in vain." He concludes that only place names have dignity, and that abstract words "such as glory, honor, courage, or hallow" are obscene. Eleven years later, Robert Jordan, referring to his participation in the Loyalist Cause as a "crusade," attempts to define how he feels:

> You felt, in spite of all bureaucracy and inefficiency and party strife something that was like the feeling you expected to have and did not have when you made your first communion. It was a feeling of consecration to a duty toward all of the oppressed of the world which would be as difficult and embarrassing to speak about as religious experience. . . . It gave you a part in something that you could believe in wholly and completely and in which you felt an absolute brotherhood with the others who were engaged in it. It was something that you had never known before but that you had experienced now and you gave such importance to it and the reasons for it that your own death seemed of complete unimportance; . . . (235).

I do not think that the fantastic disparity between Jordan's and Henry's positions can ever be adequately explained by Hemingway's reactions to world events, because I strongly doubt that political or social ideas seriously engaged him on the under-levels of his creative consciousness. As a man and as a newspaper correspondent, Hemingway was in a better position to assess European social and political developments than probably any other writer of the period. His dispatches and articles in the 1920's and 1930's are evidence that he possessed a keen political eye for what was important in the news; yet he rarely uses this material except in a superficial way, and none of his fictions are truly political. The significant line of development between the filing for a separate peace in 1929 and the return to brotherhood in 1940 can, however, be suggested on a psychoanalytic level of interpretation.

The interior struggle which is symbolized in *A Farewell to Arms* is fairly easy to follow. The tyro, Henry, undergoes a series of unjust brutalities at the hands of mysterious forces beyond his understanding. He is blown up and seriously wounded (symbolically castrated), only to be nursed back to wholeness and security by Catherine (the *anima*-mother). This idyllic union in the hospital is only a temporary stay however, (prefigured in part, by the fact of Catherine's pregnancy) and the tyro returns to the war. His opportunity for rebellion arrives during the chaos of the Caporetto retreat. His ambulance unit picks up two wandering sergeants from an engineering detachment, and when they run off, he shoots one of them, aiming at the one "who had talked the most." Neither of the sergeants is described or characterized in any detail. Henry's actual desertion takes place at the bridge when the forces of tyrannization are imaged in the merciless battle police with their "beautiful detachment and devotion to stern justice." In the face of certain execution he leaps into the water and escapes to his *anima*-mother at Stresa. There he meets Catherine and learns that the authorities have tracked him down. During the night he and Catherine escape over the lake to Switzerland where the idyl is resumed outside of Montreux. Finally Catherine dies giving birth to a still-born baby boy and the tyro is left alone in the rain.

It seems fairly clear on the psychoanalytic level that Henry's separate peace is attained at the expense of becoming an orphan and a half-man. Parricide, matricide, incest, and narcissistic suicide are clumsily ponderous terms to apply to anything as delicate as *A Farewell to Arms*, but I think it can be seen that this is what happens in the symbolic construct of the novel. Henry's wholeness is attainable only through the *anima*-mother who is from the earliest time of their meeting inexorably doomed. The father-images are split between the engineering sergeants (one of whom Henry kills for no explainable reason), the ruthless battle police, and the anonymous authorities. The tyro revolts against the tutor (symbolically killing one of his manifestations, but not all of them) and indirectly destroys his mother and *anima*. At the end of the novel he has, it is true, a separate peace with the universe, but he is bereft of any affectional contact with it.[11]

While Hemingway was writing the second draft of *A Farewell to Arms*, he learned of his own father's suicide.[12] We have every right to expect that this fact would influence the interior drama of Hemingway's fiction. The first point we notice is that, after the publication of *A Farewell to Arms*, Hemingway's fictional output noticeably slows down. *Winner Take Nothing* (1933) contains fourteen stories, and among them are some of the bitterest in the Hemingway canon: "A Natural History of the Dead," "The Mother of a Queen," "God Rest You Merry, Gentlemen." The famous *"nada"* prayer of "A Clean Well-Lighted Place" and "the opium of the people" speech of "The Gambler, the Nun, and the Radio" are in this collection. The volume is also notable for its savage concern with homosexuality and castration, and it is surely remarkable that no one of the stories has a love interest. The *anima*-mother is nonexistent, and only in "The Gambler, the Nun, and the Radio" is there a tyro-tutor relationship. In that story, however, Cayetano Ruiz is an exceptionally inadequate father image and Mr. Frazer, the tyro, concludes the action by reaching for a bottle of "giant killer" while reflecting that anything which serves as an opiate against the pain of life is a good.

The other two volumes between *A Farewell to Arms* and *To Have and Have Not* are nonfictional treatises on the pleasures of killing. In *Death in the Afternoon* (1932) not only are there long detailed descriptions of men killing bulls and bulls killing men and horses, but a rather elaborate justification for an interest in such murders:

> Killing cleanly and in a way which gives you aesthetic pleasure and pride has always been one of the greatest enjoyments of a part of the human race. One of its greatest pleasures, aside from the purely aesthetic ones . . . is the feeling of rebellion against death which comes from its administering. Once you accept the rule of death thou shalt not kill is an easily and a naturally obeyed commandment. But when a man is still in rebellion against death he has pleasure in taking to himself one of the Godlike attributes; that of giving it. This is one of the most profound feelings in those men who enjoy killing (232-33).

Green Hills of Africa (1935), which continues the interest in killing, moves from the spectator's viewpoint behind the *barrera* to the participant, Hemingway, behind the sights of a .220 Springfield. Hemingway recounts his slaughter of a wide variety of animal life, but if there is a climax to the book, it occurs in the description of a giant sable bull which got away from him, although he had gut-shot it. Both volumes with their emphasis on compulsive killing suggest that the separate peace is still in effect. In terms of our analysis it seems likely that the tyro, desperately fragmented, can only strike out again and again in repetitive acts of destruction. That the targets of his destruction are male animals of rather noble stature is not surprising; the father image has treacherously escaped the tyro by removing himself from gun-range (although he has been "gut-shot"), and the symbolic animals must fall until the oedipal fury is exhausted.

To Have and Have Not (1937)[13] marks, as we have seen, the clear recantation of the separate peace. And since social and political analysis must stumble over the abrupt switch in position, we are justified in searching the inward mechanisms of the novel for an indication of what has happened. Harry Morgan, whose prototype seems to have been invented in "After the Storm" (1932), is one of Hemingway's most brutalized characters. As tutor or father image, he is, on the one hand degraded in speech patterns, utterly lacking in dignity, and morally unscrupulous; on the other hand, his elemental power is indicated by his physical strength and endurance (his delighted lust in killing, and his admirable sexual prowess with his wife). The symbolic thrust of the novel is directed to wound-castrate him (his arm must be amputated) and finally to destroy him in a carnage of gore and pain so that the fragmented tyro may become whole. However, this has been done already in Hemingway's previous two works of nonfiction with approximately the same level of intensity, and with no obvious therapeutic value. The differences may be explained as follows. The classic formula, "A man must kill his father in order to become a man," requires not only the death of the father but the death of the son-killer and his emergence as man; in his rebirth he becomes his own father. And this is the pattern in *To Have and Have Not* which is lacking in the preceding work.

In the crucial third section of this novel, Hemingway introduces the tyro figure, Emilio, the good Cuban revolutionary. Harry Morgan, a character not overly given to sentiment or affection, thinks of him as "a kind of nice kid." Emilio voices the rebellion theme, as he explains to Harry what his movement stands for: "We want to do away with all the old politicians, with all the American imperialism that strangles us, with the tyranny of the army. We want to start clean and give every man a chance" (166). Harry listens to him tolerantly and unmoved, reflecting that "He was a nice-looking boy all right. Pleasant talking too." And then with the dispassionate efficiency of a ritual executioner, he blasts his head off. In the ensuing barrage, the three other Cubans are killed, and Harry is shot in the stomach. Like the sable bull, he is "gut-shot," but unlike the sable bull, his death has been fully propitiary. The son has become reborn in the father, and Harry's last words rejecting the philosophy of "a man alone" are the words of the son-become-father. In the chaotic, disorganized, melodramatic structure of *To Have and Have Not,* which could stand almost as an objective correlative of the disintegration of the Caporetto retreat, the tyro ceases to be a separate "piece" of the whole, and is ready for the experience of integration which is chronicled in *For Whom the Bell Tolls.*

But there are still several serious gaps in the symbolic drama. There is, as it were, a missing act between *Green Hills of Africa* and *To Have and Have Not.* And fortunately, we have three short stories, originally published in the summer and fall of 1936, which do provide the missing elements in the process of reintegration. These stories, two of which are among Hemingway's best, are "The Capital of the World" (first entitled "The Horns of the Bull"), "The Snows of Kilimanjaro," and "The Short Happy Life of Francis Macomber." We have already looked in some detail at one of them, and "The Capital of the World" is easily disposed of in terms of this discussion. The tyro hero of that story, Paco, is killed in a fight with a symbolic bull (butcher knives strapped to a kitchen chair) which in turn must be a symbolic father. He sacrifices himself with the same kind of naïve idealism that Emilio, the Cuban revolutionary, entertained; and, like Emilio, he dies "as the Spanish phrase has it, full of illusions." In Hemingway's writings which precede "The Capital of the World," the tyro does the killing exclusively; here it is sacrifice rather than destruction which is emphasized, which indicates that the movement away from the separate peace has commenced.

Both "The Snows of Kilimanjaro" and "The Short Happy Life of Francis Macomber" introduce new elements into the drama. In both, the tyro is dead at the end of the story; in both cases he dies "full of illusions"; and in both stories he symbolically shucks off his past self to emerge a new man. The new radical factor which is introduced in these stories is the "bitch-heroine" or the "wicked-mother" figure, a character only very vaguely prefigured in Hemingway's earlier fiction (specifically in several of the stories of *In Our Time*), and nowhere else evident after 1936 except in concealed form in the character of Pilar in *For Whom the Bell Tolls*. "The Short Happy Life of Francis Macomber" is a clear portrait of the dramatic changes in Hemingway's world of fantasy projection, signalizing the establishment of a new perspective on which the later mergence and emergence of the tyro can be based.

The Macomber marriage, Hemingway tells us, has "a sound basis of union. Margot was too beautiful for Macomber to divorce her and Macomber had too much money for Margot ever to leave him."[14] The action of the story will effect a decisive break in this unhealthy union, as it will also unmask to the tyro the identity of his real antagonist, the mother-image, and pave the way for a reconciliation with the father. The locale of the story—a safari in the African jungle—is unprecedented in Hemingway's landscapes as a fictional setting, and is highly appropriate for the tropical depths of awareness from which the story rises. The action opens with Macomber repeating Hemingway's unsuccessful attempts with the giant sable bull in *Green Hills of Africa;* Francis "gut-shots" a lion and then runs in cowardice from its retaliatory charge. He suffers the contempt of tutor-father Wilson, and of wicked-mother Margot, as well as his own overwhelming self-disgust. Note, though, that this action is an exact parallel of the declaration of a separate peace in *A Farewell to Arms*, viewed with an entirely different system of emotional valuation. In 1929 the failure to deal masterfully with authority and the flight from it were transformed into acts of heroic nobility. Frederick Henry's final isolation at the end of the novel was treated lingeringly as a particularly poignant result of blindly malicious injustice. Now blame has been transferred from the impersonal "world" to the self-conscious tyro, signalling the first stage in a return to health and creativity.

The immediate consequences of Francis' failure with the lion are Margot's rejection and betrayal of him with father-image Wilson and the completion of Francis' self-disgust and thorough alienation. He is now in the situation of the Hemingway of *Death in the Afternoon* and *Green Hills of Africa,* but without the temporary recourse to random killing. He hates Wilson, but he cannot act on that hatred because of his own sense of fear and unworthiness. In the chase after the bull buffaloes, he dramatically loses his fear in his hatred and performs meritoriously with the buffalo—becoming a reborn man. The denouement to the drama is inevitable. In his second facing of the wounded buffalo's charge, when it is clear that he will react like a *man,* Margot blasts his brains out with a 6.5 Mannlicher (Man-licker?). But here, as in "The Snows of Kilimanjaro," the true villain, the mother, has been exposed; and the separation between tyro and mother is healthily effected.

Macomber's relationship to Wilson has also been clarified. The father has been taught to respect the son, and the son can afford to feel brotherly affection for the father. Interestingly, there is no specific father image in "The Snows of Kilimanjaro." The mountain top, hitherto unapproachable because of Harry's gangrenous unworthiness, seems to fulfill Wilson's function on a more exalted plane. And the hyena, hermaphroditic and vicious, which we observed to be an extension of Helen, becomes even more closely identified with the "wicked-mother" figure. In sum, the self-realization of the tyro can come only when he has become man enough to tear himself free from dependence on the mother. Then, and only then, can he face his father on equal terms, symbolically becoming one with him. "The Snows of Kilimanjaro" and "The Short Happy Life of Francis Macomber" crystallize this orientation in Hemingway's fantasy-life and, on a psychological level, make Harry Morgan's recantation of the separate peace understandable. It remains only to carry this discussion through Hemingway's later fiction in order to complete the arc of its inner struggle.

For Whom the Bell Tolls is something of an anomaly in Hemingway's fiction. It is far and away his longest sustained prose narrative, it is thickly populated for a Hemingway novel, and it is creatively agile in its handling of space and shifting of backgrounds. In terms of our argument it seems significant that the writing pace was extremely fast and regular (the book took almost exactly eighteen months to write and revise);[15] it seems fair to assume that the "inner-breakthrough" of 1936-37 had released Hemingway's creative powers in great prolificity after a dry period of almost ten years. Further, the style of *For*

Whom the Bell Tolls is much more freely flowing than the brittle staccato periods which had been characteristic of Hemingway's prose. And, most significantly, it is, with the possible exception of *The Old Man and the Sea*, Hemingway's most serene work. There are scenes of violence and horror, to be sure, but these are narrated at a distance. Pilar's description of the slaughter of the Fascists and Maria's account of her parents' murders and of her own violation are violent memories recollected in something that approaches tranquillity. Even El Sordo's stand on the mountain top is placed at a narrative distance from the reader, since it is viewed by the impersonal narrator and describes the fate of a guerrilla band only peripherally connected with the main characters of interest. It would be too much to suggest that this novel is a pastoral idyl, but it is true that the emotional center of the fiction—in sometimes jarring contrast to the action described—is almost from the very beginning resonant with a harmony that is in perfect accord with Jordan's previously quoted speech on "communion," as well as with the Donnean echoes of the title. Indeed, it is even worth wondering whether the complete quotation from which the title derives—"No man is an *Island*, intire of it selfe; every man is a peece of the *Continent* . . . I am involved in *Mankinde.*" —is, as it is usually considered, a justification for taking part in a foreign war. What seems more likely to me, it is Hemingway's announcement of his achieved "at-one-ment" in himself.

At any rate, such is the way the novel reads on its lower levels; it is a happy fairy tale where all the seeming evils only appear to be evil, and all the goods gain in radiance as the novel progresses. The disasters at the end are merely the inevitabilities of death, and since life has been telescoped into a seventy-hour period, death can be accepted with an almost-Whitmanesque readiness:

> There is no such thing as a shortness of time, though. You should have sense enough to know that too. I have been all my life in these hills since I have been here. Anselmo is my oldest friend. . . . Agustin, with his vile mouth, is my brother, and I never had a brother. Maria is my true love and my wife. I never had a true love. I never had a wife. She is also my sister, and I never had a sister, and my daughter, and I never will have a daughter. I hate to leave a thing that is so good (381).

And these statements which the tyro figure makes are, in terms of the symbolic inner drama, perfectly true. The good father, Anselmo, has become his oldest friend; the bad father, Pablo, has repented of his treachery and become a helper. The gypsy witch mother, Pilar, has refrained from capturing him in the domineering nets of bad incest, and has metamorphosed into the fairy godmother, bestower of all blessings. In that role she gives him his *anima*-mother, Maria. The inner drama achieves such a harmony of relationships that "drama," a word which denotes a system of tensions, is probably inaccurate; it would be better to characterize the psychoanalytic area of action as the inner *tableau*.

The last two fictions can be treated much more cursorily. Ten years elapsed between the publication of *For Whom the Bell Tolls* and *Across the River and Into the Trees*. It is worth remarking that in that period Hemingway began to refer to himself as "Papa." We have already noticed the effects of "the symbolic doubling" in the 1950 novel. The tyro, Richard Cantwell, becomes his own father-image, projecting his *anima* into the noble mother, Renata. Characteristically, this results in Cantwell's being forced to attack himself in lieu of an external antagonist, and this he does through the device of the cardiac condition. This novel, which is the most static of all Hemingway's fiction, is largely composed of the tyro father's self-beratements and self-defenses. It does not make for good fiction, but it is extremely interesting as a relatively naked exposure of the drama beneath the drama.

And finally, as we suggested earlier, *The Old Man and the Sea* (1952) completes the cycle of the arc. Santiago is father tyro, the sea is *anima*-mother, and the boy is a displaced remembrance of the hero as a young man. The antagonist, the male marlin, is Santiago's brother, and the parable of maturity or age is cast in fresh poetic terms. The ultimate regression of the psyche to immersion in the primordial is given an authoritative and substantive treatment. There are the scavenger sharks and the Portuguese men of war to disrupt the surfaces of unity and peace; but these are merely the last thrashings of life which, in time, will subside and submerge themselves into the great boundless all.

Two concluding items should be re-emphasized. Psychoanalytic criticism of this type is useless as a measurement of the value of a work of art. In fact, it is generally more fruitful with works of inferior value, as with *To Have and Have Not* and *Across the River and Into the Trees*. Its discovery of concealed "meanings" does not at all negate other equally valuable "meanings" in the interpretation of a fiction. And above all, it does not yield anything except the most misleading information about the personality of the creator of the fiction. It is subjective in its reading, forced to deal with a bundle of unassimilated material that has already been pressed into a design for completely other purposes; and it must remain ignorant of the multitude of sensations which are a part of the artist's personality and which are never made manifest in his work. Dealing with Hemingway in particular, a man whom we have seen to pride himself on his role playing, we must remember that we can see only what he chooses for us to see; and we must also remember that he is not beyond "hoaxing" the reader for his own sense of satisfaction. Santiago may have gone back to his shack to dream of the lions on the beach, but Hemingway was still at war with the world—and the world was frequently his audience.

But this kind of analysis can be useful as one among many tools in hypothesizing a direction or a focus of examination in which the concealed springs of the creative fountain may show themselves. The single point that seems to me to be worth the discussion is the evidence which suggests that Hemingway's fiction is consistently concerned with the metaphors of his own consciousness; that his characters are intensely felt, partial projections of his own internal war: that their conflicts are less the actions of human beings in society contending with one another, than they are a delicate recording of the wracking ambiguities by which man is always on the verge of being rent asunder. Hemingway, in short, is a writer of romances; perhaps the most realistic writer of romances of all times, but a romancer nonetheless. And the value of his metaphors depends on his ability to make his poetic vision move his readers toward their own discovered truths about themselves. This point is worth retaining because it allows us to approach his fictions for what they are and not for what even he may have pretended them to be.

CHAPTER 4

The Structures of the Fiction

I

IN THE PREVIOUS CHAPTER we examined the standard
Hemingway characters whose shifting interrelations compose
the designs of the Hemingway myth. We saw that the tyro and
the tutor figures, with their protean capacities to "split" or
"double" themselves, were central to the typical Hemingway
fiction; and that even in those cases where one existed without
the other ("The Snows of Kilimanjaro," "The Undefeated"),
the presence of the missing figure was strongly implied or
symbolized. We shall make a new approach, then, to the tutor-
tyro constellation in order to investigate more pointedly the
structure of the typical Hemingway story; and we may find
that this examination will enable us to see more clearly how
Hemingway's life-view becomes refracted and brought to focus
in his establishment of *form*.

There are, I suppose, three characteristic Hemingway stories:
those in which the tyro appears more or less alone; those in
which the tutor dominates the space of the fiction; and those in
which the tutor-tyro axis regulates the revolution of the story.
We have already, in one context or another, dealt with fictions
of all these types, so we are well prepared to look at them from
a different angle. As an introductory summary we can offer
the following formula: The tyro story is an exposition of severe
emotional reaction, with the tension of the story dependent on
the contrast between the accumulated momentum of the emotion demanding to be released and the resisting forces within
the style and content which attempt to restrain that release. The
tyro story thus tends to resemble an unexploded bomb in im-
minent danger of explosion. The tutor story has a greater degree
of narrative distance and therefore depends less for its effect on

the creation of an immediate emotional impact. It is a form of exemplary story with the developed tensions released along the channels of pathos. Its direction will move inevitably toward the genre of the fable and the parable. And the tutor-tyro story follows the structure of the educational romance or, as it has been called, the "epistemological story," that characteristically American variation on the *Bildungsroman* (which is too loosely termed an "initiation" or "rites of passage" story). Its direction tends to lead to a revelation of "truth," generally in the form of self-discovery or self-realization. These three forms are, of course, not that distinct and arbitrary in Hemingway's work, and there is a constant infiltration of one form into the other.[1]

The tyro stories, in their purest form, are those Nick Adams stories in which there are no other significant characters except Nick. These would include "Big Two-Hearted River: Parts I and II," "Now I Lay Me," and "A Way You'll Never Be." "Now I Lay Me" is a straight first-person narration, while the other two are presented from an impersonal third-person viewpoint so closely focused on the tyro character as to make the narrative device very similar to James's use of a "lucid reflector." In terms of Nick's biography, "Now I Lay Me" (1927) comes first; a direct recounting of his convalescence in Milan after the Fossalta wound, it deals largely with his almost Proustian inability to go to sleep and with the various ways he diverts his mind from dangerous preoccupations that might carry him over the thin edge. The last full third of the story records the banal dialogue between Nick and a wounded fellow soldier, John. The dialogue, largely composed of John's encouragement to Nick that he should marry, is meant to serve as an ironic contrast to the restrained terrors in Nick's mind which John knows nothing about. The story doesn't quite work, however, although the straight interior memory passages are excellent; for the two sections of the story never quite engage each other. The first section is narrated with an interest that diverts the reader's attention from the state of Nick's mind to his memories themselves; and the second section has perhaps too flatted a key to provide the necessary contrast. We are meant to feel, I think, that Nick is in a far other country than the more prosaic, less sensitive John; this is one of Hemingway's recurrent themes, but I do not find it successfully dramatized within the texture of the prose.

"A Way You'll Never Be" (1933), second in the Nick chronology, deals with his shell-shocked return to his outfit after his release from the hospital. His nerves are shattered and his mind has a tendency to jump around and off, as though its flywheel were disconnected. There is some experimentation with stream-of-consciousness exposition, valuable for what it tells us about Nick; but these sections are not so selectively controlled as those in "The Snows of Kilimanjaro" and in *For Whom the Bell Tolls.* In spite of the tone of the story—and there is more obvious hysteria in it than anywhere else in Hemingway's fiction—it fails to create a meaningful tension. There just simply isn't any real conflict in the plot, the structure, or the style to make this a potential bomb. The best part of the story—a part which does develop a real tension—is the description of Nick's ride over the war-pocked road to his meeting with Captain Paravicini.

"Big Two-Hearted River: Parts I and II" (1925), third in the sequence of Nick's adventures, describes approximately twenty-four hours of activity from the time Nick gets off a train in desolated Upper Michigan to hike to a suitable campsite until he calls the fishing over for the day on the following afternoon. Although the story has no plot of any significance, and nothing happens that is in any way untoward in such a fishing trip, it builds up an almost unbelievable tension and has justly been considered one of Hemingway's finest fictions.[2] It is really a *tour de force* of style, since it is almost exclusively the style which persuades the reader that Nick is in a most precarious state of nervous tension which he is desperately holding under clenched control. From having read other Nick stories, the reader may be prepared to fill in the antecedent background to this innocuous fishing trip; but even without that background the dramatic situation of the story seems obvious.

This short paragraph is fairly representative of the style in which the entire fiction is narrated:

> Nick drove another big nail and hung up the bucket full of water. He dipped the coffee pot half full, put some more chips under the grill onto the fire and put the pot on. He could not remember which way he made coffee. He could remember an argument about it with Hopkins, but not which side he had taken. He decided to bring it to a boil. He remembered now that was Hopkins' way. He had once argued about everything with Hopkins. While he waited for the coffee to boil, he opened a small can of apricots. He liked to open cans. He emptied the can of apricots out into a tin cup. While he watched the coffee on

the fire, he drank the juice syrup of the apricots, carefully at first to keep from spilling, then meditatively, sucking the apricots down. They were better than fresh apricots.

The prose style has boned action and reflection down to their simplest components, and it holds them inexorably there. The sentences are with one exception simple declarative ones—first the subject, then the predicate, first the subject, then the predicate—repeated monotonously with little variation. The short unobtrusive "He liked to open cans," echoing the locution of the previous longer sentence, is a good example of the mastery with which Hemingway implies the dramatic situation. This and the last sentence of the paragraph are the only two places in which Nick is allowed to make a value judgment in this excerpt, and both value judgments are proffered with a kind of embarrassed finality which is shocking because the emphasis of their delivery is in suspicious contrast to the banality of the judgment. With no change, this paragraph, as well as the bulk of the story, could be used to describe a fishing trip by a particularly able and articulate feeble-minded fisherman. The monotonous repetition and the lack of subordination in the sentence structure give all items equal importance, suggesting that there is no principle of selectivity or discrimination in the focus of intelligence.

However, Hemingway has carefully introduced clues to expose Nick's situation. Early in the story we are told that Nick was happy. "He felt he had left everything behind, the need for thinking, the need to write, other needs. It was all back of him." When he crawls into his tent, we are told: "He had not been unhappy all day. . . . He had made his camp. He was settled. Nothing could touch him." And later, "His mind was starting to work. He knew he could choke it because he was tired enough." It is possible that a feeble-minded person could be happy because he believes that he has arranged things so that nothing will touch him, but we cannot believe that a feeble-minded person would have a need to write, nor that he would be concerned to choke off the activities of his mind. Hence the primitive concentration on the mechanical process of the hike, the making of camp and dinner, and the fishing on the next day can only be a superimposed restraint on an inordinately active mind which is undergoing great stress. That Hemingway is able to insinuate this desperate restraint by making his prose the stylistic equivalent of that restraint is the triumph of the story.

But the story is also something more than a very successful experiment in style. As in James's "The Jolly Corner," the *things* of the fictional locale compose an allegorical frame which represents the protagonist's consciousness. In James's story, the house with its corridors and closed rooms makes a convenient setting in which his protagonist can explore his past and under-consciousness. Similarly Nick is returning to an area that he had once known well. The town is now a ghost town and the stretch of countryside immediately around it has been scorched over. Nick passes through the burnt-out places to "the good place," where he makes his camp and where nothing can touch him. But across the river "in the swamp, in the almost dark, he saw a mist rising." He looks away from it. On the next day he fishes the stream, but he does not go into the swamp where the big trout are: ". . . in the fast deep water, in the half light, the fishing would be tragic. . . . He did not want to go down the stream any further today." And he concludes that "There were plenty of days coming when he could fish the swamp."

The story operates, therefore, on two levels. On the first it describes the self-administered therapy of a badly shocked young man, deliberately slowing down his emotional metabolism in order to allow scar tissue to form over the wounds of his past experience. On another level it represents the commencement of the journey into self. But this journey is highly cautious: "He did not want to rush his sensations any." He makes sure that he has a good safe place from which to operate. He fishes first in the brightly lit part of his stream of consciousness. And even there he acts with slow, controlled care; precipitate action may frighten away the quarry he seeks, or it may even frighten off the seeker. He knows that the big fish are in the almost dark places, in the frightening mist-hung swamps of his awareness; he knows also that, if he is to find himself, it is there that he ultimately must look. Meanwhile he gathers his courage together and takes the first measured steps of exploration into the undiscovered country of his mind. There will be plenty of time to fish the swamp.

"Big Two-Hearted River" can be seen, then, as a tyro story which generates its power not from what it actually says, but from what it does not say. It is the latter, the unspoken volumes which shriek from beneath the pressure of the taut prose exposition, that expresses the emotional communication to the reader.

This technique, which we may call "the irony of the unsaid," is one of Hemingway's favorite tricks and one of his most powerful ways of transmitting the shock of emotion in prose. This common device of the miniatures of *in our time* (his earliest tyro stories) Hemingway uses to great advantage in those tyro stories which confront Nick with situations of severe violence with which he is unable to cope. Thus, in "The Killers," in "The Battler," and in "An Alpine Idyll," situations are developed of such moral outrage as to demand a comment or an indication of appropriate reaction. The situations themselves are reported impersonally and even laconically; the presentation, as in "Big Two-Hearted River," emphasizes the disparity between what has happened and what ought to be the reaction. Hemingway's artful refusal to give an overt outlet to these reactions in the events or the style of the fictions brings the crescendo of tension to a breaking point. Hemingway, like Santiago, holds his pressure on the line until he has exacted the maximum degree of strain; if he slackens it, the reader may get away; if he pulls it too tight, the line may break (as it does in "An Alpine Idyll") and the reader will be free. But when it is just right, as in "Big Two-Hearted River," the reader is caught and forced into response.

II

There are fewer examples of the tutor story in the Hemingway canon than of the other types, but at least three of them—"The Undefeated," "Old Man at the Bridge," and *The Old Man and the Sea*—are among his finer achievements.[3] We have already remarked in other connections the impulses which drive these stories in the direction of the exemplar or the fable. The tutor figure has already achieved a self-containment or self-definition before he appears in the fiction; he already *is*, and the finality of his self-acceptance removes him from the disintegrating experiences of *becoming*. When Retana asks Manuel, "Why don't you get a job and go to work?" Manuel's answer defines his position in the metaphysical universe: "I don't want to work, I am a bull-fighter." Similarly, the old man in Hemingway's Spanish War sketch possesses an equal surety about who he is, even amidst the chaos of a refugee evacuation: "I am without politics. I am seventy-six years old. I have come twelve kilometers now and I think now I can go no further." The tutor has thus already become himself, and his further engagement in life will not seriously affect what he *is*; it will only substantiate and clarify that definition; and, when his activities are figured forth in narrative, they will necessarily be saturated with a moral significance. For when the tutor is placed in a challenge situation within his scope of mastery, he will do whatever can be done in the "right" way. And "right conduct" almost always in fiction is rendered with a strong degree of ethical coercion—hence the consequent level of didacticism in all parables.

Further, the self-containment of the tutor (the *is*-ness, as it were) will move to minimize the particularizing individuality of the tutor character. Individuality in characterization is largely a property of a character's struggle for wholeness and his inability to achieve it. We may suggest that the more individual a literary character is, the more he tends to be a "grotesque"—a character whose idiosyncrasies establish the extent to which he is at odds with himself (Dickens' "originals" are a persuasive case in point). The exemplary tutors in Hemingway's fiction will tend to transcend the fixed co-ordinates of their temporal lives and become *types*, as do Manuel and the old man caught in the flooding backwash of a civil war. As types they become representative of a limited aspect of man's condition and a model of excellence within the severe restrictions that bound the possibilities of their typicalness. However, under certain conditions, a type may be further refined of his typicality, through the process of what Hermann Broch terms "abstractism," to a point of universality where the limiting boundaries of its representativeness virtually disappear. The result in an *archetype*, and the actions through which an archetype communicates its epiphany are what we call *myth*.[4] At any rate, a process something like this has happened in the transfiguration of Manuel (1925) into the figure of Santiago (1952). The system of changes may be indicated in the following processive equation: "the man of flesh and bone" (Unamuno's phrase) becomes a type (The Bullfighter—a man facing a certain kind of death) becomes the archetype Man (alone in, but not isolated from, the Universe). We will try to examine *The Old Man and the Sea* to test the accuracy of these observations.[5]

First, however, a backward glance at one of Hemingway's stories, "The Three-Day Blow" (1925), may furnish us with a critical frame of reference from which to pursue these investigations. In that early Nick story the two adolescents, Nick and

Bill, are discussing Maurice Hewlett's romantic medieval tale, *The Forest Lovers*; Nick remembers the story in terms of its erotic interest to him:

> "Yup. That's the one where they go to bed every night with the naked sword between them."
> "That's a good book, Wemedge."
> "It's a swell book. What I couldn't ever understand was what good the sword would do. It would have to stay edge up all the time because if it went over flat you could roll right over it and it wouldn't make any trouble."
> "It's a symbol," Bill said.
> "Sure," said Nick, "but it isn't practical."

The criticism here is a just description of Hemingway's firmly held conviction on the proper uses of symbolism; the symbol must be "practical" or natural. When it is satisfactorily employed it will blend unnoticeably into the commonsense flow of empirically observed relationships. Like the Mark Twain of "Fenimore Cooper's Literary Offenses," Hemingway demands that romances obey the practical laws of cause-and-effect behavior. But like Mark Twain also, his predilection for *natural* rather than *artificial* symbols did not forbid him their very conscious use. The Hemingway who wanted to get to see the world clear and as a whole—so that any part of it would represent the whole—is, as we have remarked, in a very close parallel to Emerson's ideal poet. And his comment to George Plimpton on the presence of symbolic meanings in his fictions underscores the richness of that parallel: "I suppose there are symbols since critics keep finding them. If you do not mind I dislike talking about them. . . . It is hard enough to write books and stories without being asked to explain them as well. . . . Read anything I write for the pleasure of reading it. Whatever else you find will be the measure of what you brought to the reading."[6]

The last sentence is almost a precise equivalent of Emerson's "It is the good reader that maketh the good book." We may assume, then, that the saga of Santiago is an attempt, among other things, to represent the "whole" of man's experience through a system of symbolic correspondences.

The stripped plot of *The Old Man and the Sea* is almost as clean of clinging encumbrance as the marlin's "great long white spine with a huge tail at the end." Santiago has fished the

Gulf Stream for eighty-four days without landing a fish. For the first forty days he had been accompanied by the boy, Manolo; the rest of the time he had been alone in his skiff, placing his lines with practised precision into the depths of the sea on which he floats. On the eighty-fifth day he rows somewhat farther out than he usually does, and at noon the hook of his hundred-fathom line is taken by a huge male marlin. The great fish pulls the skiff steadily to the northwest the rest of the day and all that night, and Santiago determinedly bends all his strength and accrued experience in his craft to the task of playing the fish well. This is what he was born to do; and, in doing it, he is not just *doing*, but realizing his *being*. His action takes on symbolic reverberations when Santiago humanizes and identifies with the great fish on the end of the line: "His choice [the marlin's] had been to stay in the deep dark water far out beyond all snares and traps and treacheries. My choice was to go there to find him beyond all people. Beyond all people in the world. Now we are joined together and have been since noon. And no one to help either one of us" (55).

On the afternoon of the second day Santiago gets his first sight of the fish that he has been hooked to for some twenty-seven hours when the marlin breaks the water in a long scythe-like leap. The antagonists confront one another for a split second, and then the battle of skill and intelligence against brute strength continues. For a long second night the marlin pulls the skiff steadily, while Santiago holds pressure on the line in spite of a disabling cramp in his left hand. Before dawn the marlin makes a desperate run, but he is held at the expense of painful cord cuts on Santiago's back and left hand. The fish turns east to swim with the current, and it is the morning of the third day. He begins to make his circles, and Santiago, playing him with desperate care, finally works him close enough to the boat to harpoon him at noon of the third day. He lashes the over fifteen hundred pounds of fish to his boat and prepares for the homeward journey. The winning part of the drama is concluded; for in the end the winner must take nothing.

An hour passes before the arrival of a great Mako shark which snaps a forty-pound bite of meat before Santiago is able to kill him. The bleeding marlin leaves a wide trail of attraction behind the skiff and draws the scavenger sharks to his scent. Santiago clubs at them desperately until midnight, when he loses his last weapon. The great fish is picked clean to the bone, and Santiago sails into the harbor late in the third night with the white skeleton of his catch riding high beside him. He beaches the skiff, shoulders his mast, and makes his stumbling way back to the shack. Manolo brings him coffee later in the morning, and they make plans for further fish g. The old man goes back to sleep to dream of lions playing on a beach.

This *novella* is probably Hemingway's most evocative construction, tense and clean on the surface, but suggesting myriad layers of meaning just out of reach in the murky levels fathoms beneath. I think there can be little doubt that it is meant to be a symbolic fiction, but I think it would be wrong to suppose that Hemingway fixed his meanings in the fable, expecting his readers to haul them up after him like so many weighted lobster-traps. His remark to a reporter is revealing: "I tried to make a real old man, a real boy, a real sea and a real fish and real sharks. But if I made them good and true enough they would mean many things."[7] Nor is this remark evasive. It points out that there are meanings possible in art which evade conceptualization. For, as Emerson wrote a hundred years earlier: ". . . the quality of the imagination is to flow, and not to freeze. . . . For all symbols are fluxional; all language is vehicular and transitive, and is good, as ferries and horses are, for conveyance, not . . . for homestead." *The Old Man and the Sea* should be approached, then, as a kind of open-ended allegory in which the ultimate meanings recede beyond reach; and we must retain the critical humility to let them go. This does not rid us of the obligation to catch what we can, of course; but it reminds us that a real fable will change its shape as the needs and experience of its readers change.

Structurally, the *novella* follows the traditional pattern of the quest or the journey. Santiago has an unexplainable "call" or vocation to be a fisherman and to meet the marlin in the deep water. Mythically he has no real choice in the matter; he has been ordained for this one encounter: "Perhaps I should not have been a fisherman, he thought. But that was the thing that I was born for." And this is not a quest to be taken lightly. Santiago is not just a fisherman, he is The Fisherman—the one chosen from all the others because of his superior merits of skill and character. Manolo, who suggests the superiority of Santiago's fishing abilities, hints also that the encounter will demand something more than being merely a great fisherman: "*Qué va*," the boy said. "There are many good fishermen and some great ones. But there is only you." The movement from *type* to *arche-type* is prefigured. The great marlin will not come to a great fisherman; he will only be caught by a great Man. In Emersonian terms, Santiago is valuable because he is not a fisherman, but Man-Fishing; and Santiago's soliloquies in the skiff in which he sees his profession in organic relationship to the rest of life bequeath to his ordeal something more than exceptional competence and stamina. As he rests against the bow on the second night, he welcomes the appearance of the first stars:

> He did not know the name of Rigel but he saw it and knew soon they would all be out and he would have all his distant friends.
> "The fish is my friend too," he said aloud. "I have never seen or heard of such a fish. But I must kill him. I am glad we do not have to try to kill the stars."
> Imagine if each day a man must try to kill the moon, he thought. The moon runs away. But imagine if a man each day should have to try to kill the sun? We were born lucky, he thought. . . .
> I do not understand these things, he thought. But it is good that we do not have to try to kill the sun or the moon or the stars. It is enough to live on the sea and kill our true brothers (82-83).

As he fights the fish—a solitary old man with a straw hat desolate on the great sea—he is not in any real sense alone at all. A literal cord joins him to his "brother," the fish. Other equally strong cords bind him to the "things" of nature—the sun, the moon, and the stars; the sea life and the birds; his town, his neighbors, the boy, and his past. It is as "whole" man that he meets the fish and brings him back; and it must be as Man, not fisherman, that his experience be measured.

However, even though Santiago has been "chosen" as representative champion to go on this quest, he must be put in readiness for it. For eighty-four days his endurance to withstand failure is put to the test; he must be made "definitely and finally *salao*, which is the worst form of unlucky," before his vigil is ended. And then he must go "far out," "beyond all people in the world," to find what he seeks. The quest hero must be set apart from men and from their daily pursuits—the results of the baseball games and the gossip of the men of the fishing wharves—because immersion in the regularities of the commonplace will dull his spiritual readiness. He must receive his final rites of purification far out in the wilderness, beyond the glow of lights from Havana. He must be tortured with pain and hunger and thirst; he must be reduced to naked will and the capacity to reflect. And then, when he is thoroughly ready, the last barrier is stripped off. He loses for a moment—a barely perceptible but determining moment—his precious sense of individuality. His will remains through the pure momentum of his determination, but the "he" that began the voyage becomes lost:

> You are killing me, fish, the old man thought. But you have a right to. Never have I seen a greater, or more beautiful, or a calmer or more noble thing than you, brother. Come on and kill me. I do not care who kills who.
>
> Now you are getting confused in the head, he thought. You must keep your head clear. Keep your head clear and know how to suffer like a man. Or a fish, he thought (102).

This is the final requisite for success in the quest. In this moment Santiago loses Santiago, merges into his struggle with the fish, merges into the fish and the universal struggle of life, and becomes elemental Man and quest hero.

But this successful catch, this angling vision into the heart of mysteries, can not be brought back whole to the community of men. As they must, most men spend the greatest part of their lives enwrapped in a world where prudence and practicality are the measurements of *what is*. Living within the blanketing hum of everyday reality with solid earth beneath their feet, men cannot see what they have no eyes for, nor can they understand what they have not been prepared to understand. The tourists who mistake the marlin's skeleton for that of a shark are not especially culpable; there is no reason why they should have known the difference, just as most men cannot discern the difference between the gleam in a maniac's eye and that in a saint's or a mystic's. The kind of experience which Santiago undergoes is an incommunicable one, but it is not without value to the community of men. He has been a champion of mankind for men and not for himself. He has brought back from his isolation a fragmented gift offering to his fellows, an imperfect symbol to suggest where he has been and what he found there. There are those within the community with the experience and the imagination and the necessary love to project on that skeletal symbol a feeling of the experience which it represents.

For them the world has been redeemed; a shaft of knowing has pierced like a thunderbolt into their awareness of what it is to be a man and the image of mankind has been immeasurably enhanced. And through them the experience will be filtered down to the others who are less sensitive or less prone to enflesh the mysteries. It will suffer dilution and diffusion as it is passed along, changing into legend, into folk story, into barely remembered anecdote. But the ripples of the great marlin's dive will radiate in ever-expanding circles, and each of the community of men will be the measure of what he can find there.

I have taken pains to suggest that there is no tragic quality to this myth, and that Santiago is neither saint nor martyr. He loses three hundred dollars worth of marlin, he suffers great pain and severe tribulation, but he is never shaken at his inner center by his deprivation. He is a man; he does what he is born to do; and, in doing it, he achieves *being*. He decides that he was beaten because he went out too far; but it is difficult to believe that he *is* beaten, and it was necessary for him to go out "too far" in order to catch what he had to catch. He has far too much humility to be seen as an "over-reacher," just as he has too much love for his antagonist to sit well in a Promethean role. In fact, the pervasive equanimity that is such a marked characteristic of *The Old Man and the Sea* keeps it, I think, from breaking through into the realm of great tragic poetry that rests just one layer lower beyond the reach of Santiago's harpoon.

Within the frame of the general interpretation of this story, there are many possible special readings; for Hemingway has so successfully narrated a journey and a return that almost any "incommunicable" experience may be suggested to a reader. The travail can be seen as a religious one, an introspective one, or an aesthetic one. Without at all exhausting the possibilities, I should like to investigate these three open-ended allegorical readings. The religious interpretation has certain obvious conscious referents. Santiago (St. James) was one of the Disciples of Christ; the description of the carrying of the mast from the beach to his shack is clearly meant to remind the reader of Christ under the weight of the cross; he goes to sleep after his ordeal face down "with his arms out straight and the palms of his hands up." And in the most telling reference (and to me a distinctly artificial and obtrusive one), Hemingway has him say, "*Ay*," when he sees the school of scavenger sharks. "There is no translation for this word and perhaps it is just a noise such as a man might make, involuntarily, feeling the nail go through his hands and into the wood" (118). The Christological pattern is functional, it seems to me, if it is meant to reinforce by extended tonality the archetypicality of Man's struggle for dignified survival in a non-human universe. In other words, if the Christ brought to the reader's attention in this story is the same man-god who "was good in there" in "Today Is Friday," then it is a legitimate buttressing of meaning. But I would hesitate to ascribe more significance than that to it, for I seriously doubt that theological ideas engaged Hemingway's creative consciousness any more deeply than social or political conflicts. There is something of both Christ and Faust in Santiago, but the first has been tempered of his passion, and the second has suffered a loss in his pride; Santiago is a kind of serene and loving Ahab, and Melville's "insular Tahiti, full of peace and joy," is his true spiritual home where lions gambol like lambs on the yellow beach.

The introspective journey motif which we have already witnessed in "Big Two-Hearted River" is likewise just barely evident in Santiago's voyage and return. In Jungian terms, every quest and confrontation is a discovery of self; and Santiago completes the fishing trip that Nick began twenty-seven years earlier. The murky swamp has descended to the cold dark waters six hundred feet deep in the Gulf Stream, but Santiago has the surety and humble confidence that will allow him to go far out because he can bring his "good place" along with him. He can fish the interior depths of himself for his "brother"-self since he is "whole" now and without fear of his own dark places. "Fish, I love you and respect you very much. But I will kill you dead before this day ends." But if the marlin is a "secret sharer" in Santiago's interior consciousness, so must the other creatures in and above the sea also be. Remembering that this is an open-ended allegory, we would be wise to keep from making correspondences. Yet we must note that the great Mako shark is presented on the same king-sized level as the marlin and the Man-Fishing:

> But you enjoyed killing the *dentuso,* he thought. He lives on the live fish as you do. He is not a scavenger nor just a moving appetite as some sharks are. He is beautiful and noble and knows no fear of anything.
> "I killed him in self-defense," the old man said aloud. "And I killed him well" (116-17).

There is more than one buried self in the undiscovered country of the mind. The marlin is killed "for pride" and because Santiago is a fisherman and this act makes him fully realized. The Mako shark with his eight rows of teeth is also an "other" self, but a hostile one. That Santiago can recognize his beauty and nobility and kill him with respect, as well as with enjoyment, is an indication of the man's developed wholeness. For recalling our earlier discussion of the symbolic inner drama of Hemingway's fiction, the *dentuso* is clearly a symbol of the castrating mother, another figuration of Harry's hyena and Margot Macomber. But now in the clarity of age, the mother and the father can be met and accepted with mutual respect and without fear.

And finally I should like to deal briefly with the special aesthetic interpretation of *The Old Man and the Sea,* since in many ways it serves as a summary analogue of Hemingway's concept of the artist and the artistic process. We have in other places commented on the parallels between Santiago's fishing excursion and Hemingway's image of himself as artist; a closer reading of *The Old Man and the Sea* from this standpoint makes a persuasive case for placing Hemingway firmly within the Transcendental aesthetic tradition.[8] In this reading Santiago is the artist who must go "far out" on the seas of his experience, plumb its depths with precise care and craft to capture the biggest fish in his artistic world (the artistic vision and the artistic shock), and bring what he can of it back to his readers as an offering of fellowship and as a stimulation to human excellence. One of the purest descriptions of the Transcendental aesthetic is Nathaniel Hawthorne's "The Artist of the Beautiful."[9] In that story the artist is a watchmaker who isolates himself from the community, sacrificing his health and years of youth in order to create something beautiful. He is initially motivated by his love for a girl of the village, but as his labors continue he becomes obsessed with his own search for reality. His ultimate result is a jeweled mechanical butterfly, so delicately wrought as to take on the appearance of actual life—to glow and to fly—when it comes into a human contact of proper receptivity and imagination. He delivers his symbol of beauty to his now-married ex-sweetheart to watch with placidity the total destruction of his labors when the symbol is crushed by brutal indifference and cynicism.

Except for Hawthorne's predilections for the *artificial* rather than the *natural* in his choice of plots and symbols, this story has a striking similarity to Hemingway's fable. Like the watchmaker, Santiago is isolated from men by his artistic pursuits; and, like him, he knows that the community of men will judge with two-dimensional eyes the gift that they are not worthy to receive. The marlin will be measured in terms of thirty cents a pound when no material scale can possibly gauge its weight: "Then he was sorry for the great fish . . . and his determination to kill him never relaxed in his sorrow for him. How many people will he feed, he thought. But are they worthy to eat him? No, of course not. There is no one worthy of eating him . . ." (83). But he brings the fish home even though it will become "garbage waiting to go out with the tide," because he is Man-Fishing and this is his contribution to mankind. The watchmaker, Owen Warland, reacts to his great loss in words which closely echo the triumphantly acceptant mood with which *The Old Man and the Sea* ends: "He looked placidly at what seemed the ruin of his life's labor, and which was yet not ruin. He had caught a far other butterfly than this. When the artist rose high enough to achieve the beautiful, the symbol by which he made it perceptible to mortal senses became of little value in his eyes while his spirit possessed itself in the enjoyment of the reality."

Santiago too had caught "a far other" marlin than the skeleton which is the awed talk of the fishing harbor. The bright and perfect conception and the experience of reality that are the artist's reward for his devotion and sacrifice are as far beyond the symbol which he gives to men as the shiny peak of Kilimanjaro is beyond the heat and disease of the plain. The artist's gift and his curse are to enjoy his vision in beatific fullness and to be unable to talk about it. His duty is to become one of Emerson's "liberating gods," who will cunningly practice his tricks of illusions and symbolic "suggestiveness," in order to set his readers free to create their own experiences of artistic reality. Each, as Hemingway said, is to be the measure of what he brings to the reading. "It is the good reader that maketh the good book"—and on this level the marlin's "great long white spine" becomes a symbolic referent to the *novella* which Hemingway fished out of the Gulf Stream of his own half-century of life.

The tutor story then will go in the direction of the parable or the fable. It will be instructive as an emblem of exemplary conduct, and it may even be elevating in its moral suasion.

Given Hemingway's temperamental relation to the universe, its effects will move toward pathos rather than tragedy; its philosophical attitude will be one of cosmic acceptance rather than rejection. And its mode of acceptance will be framed within a mood of quiescent resignation rather than exhilaration or joy. Technically the presentation will be bound within the ironic mode; poetic evocation and suggestion will inform the prose with an overwhelming sense of surging meanings beneath the surface level of the action. In one of Hemingway's favorite aesthetic metaphors, he wrote: "The dignity of movement of an iceberg is due to only one-eighth of it being above water." Thus the device of what we termed earlier, "the irony of the unsaid," is enlisted in the making of the tutor stories as well as the tyro ones; but it is subtly turned to new uses.

III

We must now turn to the third typical Hemingway structure—that of the tutor-tyro story. In such a story—"The Short Happy Life of Francis Macomber" and "In Another Country" are good examples—the protagonist is placed in a learning relationship to one or more characters and events which will teach him something about the nature of life; how best to live it; and also, more important, something about himself. These then tend to be stories of *growth,* and many critics have somewhat inaccurately dubbed them "initiation" stories or chronicles of the "rites of passage."

It will be helpful for our examination of this structure, as well as for our attempt to define the nature of Hemingway's achievement, to discriminate somewhat more closely between his employment of this structure and its more traditional use in such a fiction as Faulkner's "The Bear." The latter story can justly be called an "initiation" story because the protagonist, Ike McCaslin, is literally initiated into a comprehension of certain mysteries that had been hidden from him; through the process of initiation, he loses an old self and gains a new one. He is prepared for the ceremony by a mentor whose specific function is to play spiritual obstetrician to him and others like him; and, most conclusively, Ike's moment of illumination when he meets the bear is precisely equivalent to his cousin's earlier experience, and presumably to that of the others who have been found worthy.

For "initiation" and "passage" are terms taken over from anthropological studies dealing with closed tribal systems. In such systems values are considered absolute, knowable, and capable of being transmitted from one generation to another under proper conditions of incantatory sensitization. But we have found so far in our study of Hemingway that values are not absolute; that, although they are learnable, they are not teachable. In other words, the open-ended allegory, which we referred to earlier, and the carefully limited sphere of competence which Hemingway allows his professionals to be skillful within leave open the incalculable area of the unknown and the unknowable—a no-man's-land which, for Hemingway, can be dealt with only in pragmatic terms. Hence, the designation, "epistemological story," which places its emphasis on the learning process per se, seems to me to be a more accurate description.[10]

In Hemingway's stories of this type, the protagonist is always the tyro. Sometimes, as in "In Another Country," this is difficult to see; but it is always the tyro figure who encloses and structures the story. These stories are usually narrated in the first person; but, when narrated from an impersonal viewpoint, they achieve the same effect through a variation of the Jamesian device of the "reflecting consciousness." Also, since the tyro is generally in a state of stress or imbalance, this tutor-tyro story frequently merges with the straight tyro stories or "unexploded bomb" stories. "The Killers" or "The Battler," for example, might be included in this type. The distinctive feature of the epistemological story, it seems to me, is the emphasized presence within the story of a tutor figure who serves as a model of instruction for the tyro. Such a tutor must have created for himself a specific *modus vivendi* which is pertinent to the tyro's immediate emotional needs. The tyro, as we have seen in an earlier discussion, cannot become as adept as the tutor. But he can learn some partial lessons, and he can, in processive pragmatic fashion, learn who and what he is at the specific time of the learning. He can also lay plans for the immediate future. These last two points should be borne in mind because they help to explain why absolute systems are incompatible with Hemingway's vision of himself and the world. Hemingway's view of man—and this will become clearer in our discussion in the next chapter—accepts and even demands the possibility of change. Thus his epistemological stories are "growth" stories in which the new shapes of growth are unpredictable beforehand.

We will look briefly once more at "In Another Country" to get a short view of how this structure operates. And then we will take a longer view at *A Farewell to Arms* for a fuller perspective. "In Another Country" seems at first to be more of a sketch than a story. Narrated in first person by Nick Adams, it describes in seemingly random fashion his experiences undergoing rehabilitation treatment for his knee wound in Milan. He, along with other wounded, reports to the hospital every afternoon to work on the therapeutic machines. He becomes friendly with three wounded officers, all of them deservedly decorated for valor in combat; and they make it a custom to walk home from the hospital together: ". . . we felt held together by there being something that had happened that they, the people who disliked us, did not understand." It is clear that the experiences of battle and of being wounded have set the four of them off "in another country" from the people who jostle them on the streets. Similarly, the hospital is separated from the main part of the city by a network of canals; and, from whatever direction it is approached, it can only be entered by crossing a bridge. However, Nick's three friends, "the hunting hawks" who have proved their bravery, read the papers on his decorations and realize that he is not really one of them; his decorations have been given him because he is an American. He is not friendly with them after that because they have already crossed a bridge that is at the moment beyond his approach. Nick does stay friendly with a boy who was wounded on his first day at the front, because he also is not a "hawk."

It is at this point that Nick meets the Major and the events occur that we have described in Chapter III; and from this point on in the story, Nick appears to become merely a spectator-recorder of the Major's travail. But to read the story in this way is to miss Hemingway's careful construction of background in the first section. Nick knows that he would not have performed as bravely as the "hunting hawks," and he worries about his real or potential lack of bravery. Set apart by an un-recrossable bridge from the people who have not suffered the immediate violence of war, he is also set apart from those who have fought bravely and without fear: "I was very much afraid to die, and often lay in bed at night by myself, afraid to die and wondering how I would be when I went back to the front again." The Major's agony and his heroic hold on dignity under the burden of his wife's sudden death—a dignity which does not place itself above showing emotion in basic physical ways—become an object lesson to Nick which is directly relevant to his concern with bravery. The "hunting hawks" believe in bravery; it is because they do that they can reject Nick. The Major "did not believe in bravery"; he also had no confidence in the machines that were to restore his hand. He does believe in grammar, in punctuality, in courtesy, and in following the line of duty. And in the story he becomes an exemplar of courage and of dignified resolution in meeting disaster. His actions point out to Nick that a man should find things he cannot lose; that is, a man should slice away from his thoughts and convictions all the illusions that he can live without. And to Nick's immediate concern, he demonstrates that bravery is merely another illusion. He teaches Nick that there is "another country" he can enter which is open to him even with his fear. And this is a country in which unillusioned courage is a more valuable human quality than bravery.

One of Hemingway's masterful achievements in modern short-story technique is exhibited in the structure of this story. His device of "the irony of the unsaid" takes on another employment in his handling of the educational climax of Nick's studies. Nowhere does he indicate that Nick learned anything from the Major's example. Reading the story swiftly, it appears that Nick is not even present at the denouement. But from the first magnificent paragraph describing the cold autumn in Milan to the last description of the Major looking emptily out the window, the selection of every detail is controlled by Nick's mind and by his urgent concern with his fear. The power of the Major's resolution is communicated because it makes a powerful impression on Nick. Nick does not state its impression on him, probably because he has not yet synthesized his impressions into a conceptual form. But they have been synthesized in the narrative structure through juxtaposition and a repetition of the bravery theme. Hemingway once wrote proudly that he chose not to put a "Wow" at the ends of his stories: he preferred to let them end and hang fire, as it were. In a story like "In Another Country," we can see the device handled with consummate artistry. The reader is forced into a participative position; he dots the "i's" and crosses the "t's" and learns Nick's lesson simultaneously with him. At times Hemingway's use of this structure becomes so over subtle as to be entirely lost to a reader, and the story drifts away into vignette or sketch ("The

Light of the World," "Wine of Wyoming"); less frequently, the
lesson is too well learned and overly articulated at the end, and
the story becomes the text for a moralizing sermon ("The
Gambler, The Nun, and the Radio"). But in those cases where
the "wow" is deliberately withheld to create a cogent meaningful
ambiguity at the end, the tutor-tyro stories can be extremely
effective.

A *Farewell to Arms* is not generally regarded as an "epistemological story." It has been called among other things a
"tragedy," an unconvincing romance, a masterful depiction of
the impersonal cruelty of war.[11] It may be some of these other
things as well (although not, I think, a tragedy); but the key
to its structure must lie in the lesson that the total experience
has taught to Frederick Henry. It is his story which he tells in
his own voice; the meanings which are sunk in the texture of the
story can only be the meanings which he has recognized as
salient in his experience because they offer him pragmatic
hypotheses on what life *is* and, more important, who he *is*.
The total effect of the story depends on the degree of Frederick's
self-realization or acceptance of the implicit meanings in his
experience; for, as we have seen with Hemingway, the identity
of a man is measured by the processive recognitions of his
meaningful experience. A *Farewell to Arms* departs slightly from
the rigid format of the tutor-type structure in that there is no
single tutor whom the tyro, Henry, will accept. There are, however, several tutors; and, in a sense, his entire series of episodic
adventures is a composite tutorial stimulation.

The key to the motif of self-discovery occurs early in the novel
when Frederick Henry attempts to explain to the priest and to
himself why he had spent his furlough in the opiate-inducing
carnival atmosphere of the cities rather than in the priest's home
area, the Abruzzi:

> I myself felt as badly as he did and could not understand why
> I had not gone. It was what I had wanted to do and I tried to
> explain . . . winefully, how we did not do the things we wanted
> to do; we never did such things. . . . I had wanted to go to
> Abruzzi. I had gone to no place where the roads were frozen
> and hard as iron, where it was clear cold and dry and the snow
> was dry and powdery and hare-tracks in the snow and the
> peasants took off their hats and called you Lord and there was
> good hunting. I had gone to no such place but to the smoke
> of cafés and nights when the room whirled . . . nights in bed,

drunk, when you knew that that was all there was, and the strange excitement of waking . . . and the world all unreal in the dark and so exciting that you must resume again unknowing and not caring in the night, sure that this was all and all and all and not caring. Suddenly to care very much and to sleep to wake with it sometimes morning and all that had been there gone and everything sharp and hard and clear. . . . I tried to tell about the night and the difference between the night and the day and how the night was better unless the day was very clean and cold and I could not tell it; as I cannot tell it now. But if you have had it you know. He had not had it but he understood that I had really wanted to go to the Abruzzi but had not gone and we were still friends, with many tastes alike, but with the difference between us. *He had always known what I did not know and what, when I learned it, I was always able to forget. But I did not know that then, although I learned it later.* (13-14, italics added).

This lengthy excerpt is crucial, I believe, in outlining the frame of reference in which Frederick's experiences coalesce into a significant shape. We must first know, of course, what he is before his experiences begin; for it is only through measuring the distance between what he had been and what he becomes that we can know what he is at the end of the novel after he has finally learned what the priest had always known. We must also remember that the complete novel is told in one long memory-flashback; that there is a qualitative difference between Henry the narrator-protagonist and Henry the actor-protagonist in the novel. And that this difference—one in both time and knowledge—will necessarily impact a dynamic irony to the narrative perspective.

Frederick Henry's character at the beginning of the novel can be readily summarized. He is rootless; he has a stepfather somewhere in America, but he has quarrelled so much with his family that the only communication between them is in their honoring of his sight drafts. His general attitude toward life can be almost entirely abstracted from the previously quoted excerpt. Most of the time he does not care about anything at all: ". . . the world all unreal in the dark . . . and not caring in the night, sure that this was all and all and all and not caring." He has been a student of architecture, but there is no indication that this represents anything more than a casual easily dissolvable interest. He has volunteered to serve in the Italian Ambulance Corps for reasons which are never made clear. He has neither patriotism nor hatred of the Austrians. In fact, the war and his involvement in it are as unreal experiences to him as anything else in his thoroughly meaningless and unconnected life. "Well, I knew I would not be killed. Not in this war. It did not have anything to do with me. It seemed no more dangerous to me myself than war in the movies" (39). Although he has had sexual experiences with many women, none of them has lodged in any meaningful way in the designing of his person. Or, to put it in other terms, the character or *self-ness* of Frederick Henry which we meet at the beginning of the novel is practically nonexistent. He *is* his manners and his intermittent drive to satisfy his creature-instincts in drinking, sex, and the sporadic excitement of the sensations which the violence of war provides. And this central emptiness is brilliantly symbolized in the persistent image of the masquerade; he is an unrooted American disguised in an Italian uniform. Or, as Ferguson expertly perceives when she calls him a "dirty sneaking American Italian," he is "a snake with an Italian uniform: with a cape around [his] neck."[12]

However, there is another aspect to his character to which the priest responds. Although Henry represses and ignores it for the most part, he does possess a strong potential "caringness." There are times, as we see in the excerpt, when he cares a good deal; and everything becomes "sharp and hard and clear." It is this aspect of his character which grows during the novel and which serves as a force field for the development of his personality. However, in the beginning of the novel, and up to the time of the wound, this aspect is consistently and consciously smothered. "It was what I had wanted to do and I tried to explain. . . . winefully, how we did not do the things we wanted to do; we never did such things. . . ." The careful adverb, "winefully," is the exposing clue to the masquerade lie of Henry's protestations. It was *not* what he had wanted to do at all. He *wanted* to go to the cities where he could merge his excited emptiness into the empty carousings of a soldier's leave in wartime. For one of the lessons that Henry learns in the course of the novel is that people always do the things they want to do; and, when their capacity for "caring" is limited or negligible, their wants are most easily assuaged by passive activities of an instinctual nature. Somewhat later in the novel when the characterization is no longer completely true, Rinaldi acutely describes the Henry of emptiness: "You are really an Italian," he says. "All fire and smoke and nothing inside. You only pretend to be an American" (71).

Thus Henry is, in a sense, playing a double masquerade. He is to Ferguson a sneaking American hiding in an Italian uniform; to Rinaldi he is an Italian pretending to be an American. The ironies of ambiguous identity will multiply at the bridge over the Tagliamento when Henry will realize that to the battle police he will be "obviously a German in Italian uniform." But at his second meeting with Catherine Barkley he is merely "not-caringness" willing to play the game of caring if there is any prospect of an exciting reward; in other words, his attitude toward her is precisely similar to his attitude toward the war in general. We see this fact when she slaps him at the beginning of their courtship: "I was angry and yet certain, seeing it all ahead like the moves in a chess game." And then later he extends the game-playing metaphor, adding the disguise-motif: "I knew I did not love Catherine Barkley nor had any idea of loving her. This was a game, like bridge, in which you said things instead of playing cards. Like bridge you had to pretend you were playing for money or playing for some stakes. Nobody had mentioned what the stakes were. It was all right with me" (32).

In his incapacity to care he can, of course, play for any amount of stakes because he has nothing to lose. The wound is the first lesson to him of what he stands to lose. He realizes in the explosion of the trench-mortar shell that he does have a *me* that the war has something to do with: "I tried to breathe but my breath would not come and I felt myself rush bodily out of myself and out and out and out and all the time bodily in the wind. I went out swiftly, all of myself, *and I knew I was dead and it had all been a mistake to think you just died.* Then I floated, and instead of going on I felt myself slide back. I breathed and I was back" (58, italics added). The italicized segment is very curious; it seems to say that, in this moment of extreme shock, Henry realizes that he is dead and has been dead for a long time; and that the mistake is in thinking that he has just died. Such a reading would substantiate the thesis that Henry has lacked a *self* up to the time of the wound, because, in these terms, "not-caringness" is equivalent to death. But even if the italicized section is an awkwardness of construction, the effect of the nearness of death and the horror of the wound (the pain and the drip of the hemorrhaging corpse above him in the ambulance) is enough to indoctrinate that value of life which the fear of death must inevitably cause.

In the field hospital the issue is dramatically externalized in the successive visits of Rinaldi and the priest. Rinaldi, as he later describes himself, is "the snake of reason," or the rationalization of not-caringness; the priest is his opposite number, the dove of faith, the consecration of *caritas*. Rinaldi warns Frederick that love is an illusion when he perceives his friend's encroaching involvement with Catherine. He insists that he and Henry are similar inside; that neither of them entertains illusions (or "care"); hence, both are invulnerable. "I just tell you, baby, for your own good. To save you trouble." Henry does not accept the advice of his reason, but he does not reject it either.

With the arrival of the priest, the counter argument is delivered. The priest, filled with shame and disgust at the war, observes correctly that Frederick really doesn't mind the war. "You do not see it. . . . even wounded you do not see it. I can tell." In the ensuing conversation the priest diagnoses Henry's deficiency and gives the definition of care which Henry will later come to embrace with qualifications:

> He looked at me and smiled.
> "You understand but you do not love God."
> "No."
> "You do not love Him at all?" he asked.
> "I am afraid of him in the night sometimes."
> "You should love Him."
> "'I don't love much.'"
> "Yes," he said. "You do. What you tell me about in the nights. That is not love. That is only passion and lust. When you love you wish to do things for. You wish to sacrifice for. You wish to serve."
> "I don't love" (76-77).

The issue has been drawn; and, although Frederick will come to a balance somewhere between Rinaldi and the priest, the rest of the novel will be an uninterrupted progress away from Rinaldi.

Book Two records the consummation of the affair with Catherine and the idyllic union they share in the four or so months of Henry's convalescence. According to the priest's definition of love, there is little doubt that Catherine achieves it: "I want just what you want. There isn't any me any more. Just what you want." But Henry's position is more difficult to determine. He "loves" Catherine, worries about not having married her when he learns that she is pregnant, and certainly enjoys her serviceable company. During his stay in the hospital, he centers on the island of pleasure and fulfillment which she fashions for him in the midst of the war. But his role is consistently that of the accepter of services; nowhere is there any indication that he is moved to become servitor as well as master. She creates the various "homes" they occupy, and at the termination of his treatment she remains outside the railway station, while he entrains to return to the front.

Book Three returns Frederick to the front and to the persuasive ministrations of his two friends, both of whom have fared badly under the strain of the summer offensives. Rinaldi fears that he has contracted syphilis (a traditional disease of lust); and, incapable of believing in anything not measurable by the empirical reason, he has buried himself in his work to avoid seeing the carnage and degradation that he works within. Henry is offered an insight into the inner life of his friend without illusions when Rinaldi, drunk, bitter, and a little hysterical tries to goad the priest into an argument: " 'No, no,' said Rinaldi. 'You can't do it. You can't do it. I say you can't do it. You're dry and you're empty and there's nothing else. There's nothing else I tell you. Not a damned thing. I know, when I stop working'" (185).

The priest, on the other hand, has also become depressed in his faith by the action of the war. He had believed in some kind of miracle which would intercede and cause men to lay down their arms, but now he has begun to doubt his belief. When he asks Frederick what he believes in, Frederick tells him, "In sleep." The answer receives an ironic doubling when Frederick apologizes: "I said that about sleeping, meaning nothing." The ironic slip may have been unconscious on Frederick's part, but it suggests that his capacity to care has not yet moved into the domain of the priest's definition.

The rest of Book Three takes Frederick into the Caporetto retreat, his vain attempt to save his ambulance crew and follow out his orders, and his climactic jump from the bridge into the Tagliamento. Yet his actions throughout this book still maintain the *passive*, moved-about quality that we observed in his character before his meeting with Catherine. He deserts at last, but only because he has been pushed to the wall. And, as he rides the flatcar to Mestre, he reflects: "I was not made to think. I was made to eat. My God, yes. Eat and drink and sleep with Catherine. . . . and never going away again except together. Probably have to go damned quickly. She would go." There is probably a fractional move closer to a commitment to a *mutual* love relationship indicated here, but it should be noted that "the separate peace" is filed by Henry neither as an action through which he can rejoin his beloved, nor as an act of disillusionment with the ideals of war. As we saw earlier, he never had any of these ideals to start with; and we can suppose that, had there been no battle police on the bridge, he would not have left his unit at this time.

In Book Four, Frederick's course is confirmed. Moved by circumstances beyond his control, he accepts the consequences of his forced actions, among them the obligations of *caring* for Catherine in the priest's sense. On the train for Stresa, he feels like a "masquerader" in his civilian clothes, which is an ironic turnabout, because he is now going to Catherine as *himself* wholly for the first time. The extent to which he has allowed himself to be penetrated by his openness for her can be seen in the following reflection:

> Often a man wishes to be alone and a girl wishes to be alone too and if they love each other they are jealous of that in each other, but I can truly say we never felt that. We could feel alone when we were together, against the others. It has only happened to me like that once. I have been alone while I was with many girls and that is the way that you can be most lonely. But we were never lonely and never afraid when we were together. I know that the night is not the same as the day: that all things are different, that the things of the night cannot be explained in the day, because they do not then exist, and the night can be a dreadful time for lonely people once their loneliness has started. But with Catherine there was almost no difference in the night except that it was even better time (266-67).

In terms of the earlier discussion, the Frederick who meets Catherine at Stresa has gone to Abruzzi; and, in his caring, things have become "sharp and hard and clear" to him. Later in his conversation with the aged Count Greffi, he answers the latter's question as to what he values most by saying "Some one I love." And the Count, who is worried because he has not become devout in his old age, brings the priest's definition to bear on Frederick's new feeling when he tells him that his being in love is "a religious feeling." The game that Frederick had entered so blithely some six months before has become a game which he cannot back out of, and the stakes are very high. In the escape across the lake to Switzerland, the "separate peace" has become a separate "union," and the way is prepared for the fulfillment of Rinaldi's earlier prophecy that the "caring"-Henry would have a better time than he, but he would also suffer more remorse (181).

Book Five moves swiftly to its inevitable catastrophe. The interlude of waiting outside Montreux brings the separate "union" to its apotheosis; the move to Lausanne and the brilliantly handled hospital scenes leave Frederick Henry "saying good-by to a statue," which is all he has left of his gamble with love. In the rain, the persistent symbol of foreboding in the novel, he returns alone to his hotel, a winner who is taking nothing away from the gaming table but a "self" vulnerable to the hurts of the world. For we must realize that there are two opposite movements in the novel, and to neglect one of them is to throw the delicate ambiguity of the novel's balance awry. On the one hand, there is the current of doom—the inexorable march of tragic warning which is echoed in the imagery, the rain, and the narrator's prescient comments. It is this movement, presumably, which Hemingway must have been referring to when he termed *A Farewell to Arms* his *Romeo and Juliet*.[13] And I suppose it is his *Romeo and Juliet*, although it bears very little resemblance to Shakespeare's. Frederick and Catherine do not fall in love at first sight; it is only very gradually that Frederick allows himself to be exposed to a real love; Catherine's death may be "a dirty trick," but it is not accidental; it is eminently natural. To compare Hemingway's lovers to those other "star-crossed" ones tells us little about Shakespeare and forces an unjust criticism of Hemingway's more limited success.

For the other movement in the novel is one in which there is no precedent in Shakespeare's tragedy. Frederick Henry establishes a connection with the world in his love affair with Catherine and, in so doing, becomes humanly alive. That she dies does not negate his experience; it pushes him into the position of the Major who also had trouble in resigning himself. Frederick moves from the safety of the half-man who has found things that he cannot lose, to the precarious and highly vulnerable position of the man who has made an investment in life and must learn to back his play. And that he does learn to resign himself is obvious in the fact that it is he, not an impersonal narrator, who tells the story. As is the case with "In Another Country," Hemingway does not spell out the process of adjustment that Frederick goes through in order to learn to endure his loss. He leaves the significant facts in the narrative structure; they are there because the narrator Frederick has abstracted them from the actor Frederick's experience. And these tell us that Frederick does not return to the Rinaldi position where there is nothing but emptiness and dryness underneath; nor does he embrace the faith of the priest. He accepts the reality of the naturalistic world in which death is a fact every bit as real as sex; but he also accepts the reality of a love which he helped to create, and this fact is also as real as death. And, as a final gloss on the novel, we may find a small substantiation in the title. *A Farewell to Arms* is beautifully ambiguous in two obvious realms: the farewell to war in the separate peace, the farewell to the beloved in death. But it also may suggest a farewell to those arms which the early Frederick Henry had opposed to the world: a farewell to "not-caringness" which gives a death-in-life to which no one can resign himself.

CHAPTER 5

The Code: A Revaluation

I

OUR DISCUSSION of *A Farewell to Arms* raises several
interesting questions concerning the Hemingway "code" and
suggests that the code is somewhat more complicated than it at
first appears to be. We noticed that, although Frederick Henry
obviously learned a good deal from his experience, he did not
embrace any single code from one of his professional tutors.
He rejects Rinaldi's stance toward life, and he also rejects that
of the priest. Similarly we can see that Mr. Frazer in "The
Gambler, the Nun, and the Radio," does not embrace the way
of life represented by the Mexican gambler, Cayetano Ruiz,
although he respects and admires Cayetano's capacity to restrain
and control his responses in a very painful situation. Even the
most famous code learner in Hemingway's fiction, Francis
Macomber, cannot be described as a disciple of Wilson in the
usual sense; certainly there is no likelihood that, had Francis
survived his safari, he might have become a white hunter. And
yet all these protagonists do learn something from their fictional
experiences and are able to apply their knowledge in a practical
manner to the way they live their lives. All of them do become
recipients of something that is usually called "the Hemingway
code." In order to understand more accurately the implications
of this code, we will have to retrace our steps slightly to revaluate
its significance in relation to the whole focus of Hemingway's
work.

At the risk of making this more confusing than it need be,
it may be helpful to think of there being two Hemingway codes,
not one. There is obviously the notorious sportsman's code of so
much hostile Hemingway criticism: the ethic of the professional
which applies to the areas in which he operates, be that soldiery,

prostitution, gambling, or deep-sea fishing. This code, in what-ever area of violent or non-violent sport it covers, can be easily understood. It is that system of arbitrary "thou shalt not's" which comprises the rules which govern professional activity within the particular sport. The hunter does not shoot at game from moving vehicles; the bullfighter does not win glory in killing unless he goes in with his sword over the horns; the gambler does not tell the police who shot him; the soldier does not disobey orders even when he is convinced that his superior officers are stupid.

First, as is frequently pointed out, these various systems which make up the professional code are really extensions of juvenile and adolescent game playing, in which the imposition of "rules" serves the purposes of making a game more interesting ("fun") to play since there will be a designed "order" to constitute a challenge for the player. And, second, the rules provide a hierarchy of valuation ("morality") by which the achievement of the individual player may be measured. The best fisherman is not the man who brings in the biggest or the most fish; a hand-grenade exploded in a small pond will do that. The best fisherman is the one who plays the fish according to the rules which impose the highest degree of challenge on the fisherman without cancelling out his chances for success. And since most sports are followed for the pleasure of the challenge rather than for the material success (the dead fish, birds, etc.), the rewards of victory are measured in terms of sports-code morality. Skill, endurance, courage, and honor are some of the characteristics which this code is equipped to evaluate.

As we discussed earlier, the sports code also functions as a pragmatic program for prediction within the area defined by the rules. The player knows in advance what is expected of him in the game he is to play; he does not know what combination of challenges are likely to converge on him at any single time. Through training and experience in his sport, he can learn a set of automatic (almost reflex) responses to a broad variety of differing challenges, although he must always bear in mind the uniqueness of every individual challenge. When a player's skill is developed to a high degree and when his accumulated experience in the game is wide enough to give him a substantial backlog of unique challenges from which to make generalizations, he can be called a "professional." When, on top of that, he possesses confidence enough in his ability to predict quickly and to act resolutely in the face of the challenge, he is likely to be a good professional.

And finally, if the nature of that particular sport in which he engages is such as to include the physical risk of his own life, reputation, or property when he is clumsy or inept in his judgment, and if he possesses all of the above-listed qualifications *plus* the courage to control his natural fear at the thought of the possible consequences, then for Hemingway he is a great and enviable professional. And his rewards will consist of his satisfaction in being able to do a difficult thing well, his transferred confidence to areas outside his field of mastery, and the emotional thrill which is concomitant with the act of meeting a demanding challenge with grace and adequacy.

But this sportsman's code is not the Hemingway code. We noticed earlier that all of Hemingway's professionals do not act well within and outside their areas of supposed competence. Pablo in *For Whom the Bell Tolls* is disgusted to discover that the Fascist priest does not die well; the *Gran Maestro* is incompetent in those discussions with Colonel Cantwell that move into the areas of higher strategy; and the successful bullfighter in "the Mother of a Queen" is less than adequate in his responses to normal sexual demands and to his obligations to his dead mother. Neither Hemingway nor his characteristic tyro protagonists are really concerned with the sportsman's code, although it provides useful metaphors and dramatic illustrations for the workings of the real code.

We have seen that life is imaged consistently in terms of a game for Hemingway, but the game is like none that was ever played for sport. The rules are very simple: man the player is born; life the game will kill him. The code which does concern Hemingway and his tyros is the process of learning how to make one's passive vulnerability (to the dangers and unpredictabilities of life) into a strong, rather than a weak position, and how to exact the maximum amount of reward ("honor," "dignity") out of these encounters.

In a famous comment in *Death in the Afternoon,* Hemingway wrote: ". . . all stories, if continued far enough, end in death, and he is no true story-teller who would keep that from you." The Hemingway code is the ethic, or philosophic perspective, through which Hemingway tries to impart *meaning* and *value* to the seeming futility of man's headlong rush toward death. And, as we shall attempt to demonstrate, the Hemingway code does more than erect a barrier of resignation, or stoicism, between man's struggles and ultimate failures. It also provides for a significant measure of *freedom* for human actions within which morality can operate and human responsibility can be judged in terms of *active* rather than *passive* responses. This final point should be carefully examined because its neglect will inevitably distort Hemingway's considered stance toward life into either an ephebic code of primitive bravery or a desperate style of abject surrender.[1]

To place it in its simplest terms, let me suggest that the real Hemingway code—what it is that his tyro figures painfully learn and relearn—consists of two lessons: the ability to make realistic promises to oneself, and the ability to forgive oneself one's past. Both of these capacities can be found analogically within the sportsman's code, but their transference into a life-attitude removes them far beyond the juvenile restrictions of "playing the game" and "being a good sport." It makes them, in fact, as viable an attitude to bring toward life in any of its aspects— domestic, social, and philosophical—as any other religiously or humanistically oriented twentieth-century life philosophy. That Hemingway frequently dramatized this perspective in the activity of violent games should not conceal the fact that the perspective was created to operate meaningfully in just one violent game— the game of life. More misunderstanding and conscious or unconscious distortion of Hemingway's position has accrued about this single point in Hemingway's philosophic perspective than around any other aspect of his fiction. It is, therefore, crucial to a just appreciation of his achievements that we apprise ourselves of what the code actually is and how and why it is designed to function.

II

The creation of the code is such a persistent preoccupation in the entire course of Hemingway's fiction that no single work gives it a full illustration. A good introduction into its form and subtleties, however, may be found in that magnificent story which Edmund Wilson called "a five-page masterpiece"—"A Clean Well-Lighted Place" (1933). This story is unusual in the Hemingway canon since it departs from the typical structures we discussed in the last chapter; there is no clear tyro figure (unless it is the older waiter) and no clear tutor figure (unless it is the old man). In this one instance, Hemingway seems to have given rein to his poetic vision and to have contented himself with the casting of an indelible image in which placement and chiaroscuro function as dramatic entities (Sean O'Faolain calls this "an almost-silent movie"). The story has the symbolic resonance of a fable; but, unlike *The Old Man and the Sea*, it is a fable without a fixed referential base. To continue the terms earlier employed, "A Clean Well-Lighted Place" is an allegory which is open on both ends.

Nothing dramatic occurs in the story; the setting is almost all there is. It is very late at night in a simple Spanish café; the only customer is an old man who had made an unsuccessful suicide attempt a week before. The two waiters in the café—one young, the other older—discuss the old man; and the younger waiter, eager to get home, closes up the place despite the older waiter's objections.[2] The older waiter muses on such matters as the difference between a well-lighted café and an all-night *bodega*, the problems of age, and the difficulties of getting to sleep when one has nothing to attach oneself to: "What did he fear? It was not fear or dread. It was a nothing that he knew too well. It was all a nothing and a man was nothing too. It was only that and light was all it needed and a certain cleanness and order. Some lived in it and never felt it but he knew it was all *nada*. . . ." Then the old waiter recites the Lord's Prayer, substituting the word "*nada*" for all the important verbs and nouns; has a cup of coffee at a *bodega*; and prepares to return to his room to toss wakefully until dawn comes.

The story radiates its meaning around Hemingway's ability to make the experience of *nada* ("nothingness") palpable and convincing to the reader. The nothingness of the fable would include everything that exists outside of the "clean well-lighted place." The nothing is everywhere, "so huge, terrible, overbearing, inevitable, and omnipresent that, once experienced, it can never be forgotten."[3] It is characterized by an absence of order, an absence of light, an absence of meaning. It is, in pure and ominous terms, the chaos of non-meaning—primordial and ineffaceable—which, for Hemingway, exists in its most concentrated and terrifying form at the point of the still moment of time in which the human *will* is challenged to make a response. T. S. Eliot gives a graphic description of that moment in "The Hollow Men" (1925):

Between the idea
And the reality
Between the motion
And the act
Falls the Shadow

For Thine is the Kingdom

Between the conception
And the creation
Between the emotion
And the response
Falls the Shadow

Life is very long

Between the desire
And the spasm
Between the potency
And the existence
Between the essence
And the descent
Falls the Shadow

For Thine is the Kingdom

But there is a distinctive difference between Eliot's presentation and Hemingway's. The "shadow" which falls on the still moment of time in Hemingway's description is not a presage, even connotatively, of theological existence. Hemingway's fiction, at least, does not take place "in His Kingdom," and the pragmatic code that he erected and clung to is without spiritual sanctions or sanctifications. A successful passage across the "shadow" is the test of all ethical and moral codes. In fact, moral codes exist largely to function as guides of the passage. A comparison of Hemingway's mode of passage with that of traditional religious philosophy ought to highlight the differences between Hemingway's faith in a clean well-lighted place and Eliot's.

The still moment of time—the moment in which human beings make decisions—exists, in terms of morality, *sui generis*, outside of time, within the space of its own creation. On the other hand, it is the product of all past time that ever was; and it is the genesis of all future time that ever will be. Any code of morality which attributes the freedom of responsible choice to human behavior will reject the notion of a completely deterministic past, for such a notion would make morality irrelevant and human beings not responsible for their acts and failures to act. But our empirical sense (whether the commonsensical variety or the scientific code of philosophical naturalism) is a persuasive agent in demonstrating to us that the past in its inexorable continuum does determine the future and does control the passage across the shadow.

From a human viewpoint this suggests that the shadow is meaningful only as a manifestation of physical principles at work; that man's dearly held values (love, justice, courage, etc.) are sheer illusions and that his attempt to act with dignity (he who is but a bundle of externally motivated responses) is a rather pitiful joke. This is the great dilemma for the modern artist: are values jokes or are they worthy of belief? Is there meaning in this chaos of seeming non-meaning (*nada*) or not? And with the failure of modern religion to supply a deeply convincing rationale in which man can trust to a Providence beyond his understanding to make a super-sense out of what appears to be non-sense, modern man's attempts to effect a passage across the shadow have stimulated some of his most unnerving reflections and, peripherally, some of his most intense creations of art. As we can guess from the excerpt from Eliot's poem, Eliot will move out of the shadow by embracing a theological sanction for the passage which removes it to a non-empirical dimension of grace. Hemingway's code is an attempt to cross the passage by creating a dimension of meaning within the naturalistic flow of physical events, but without invoking a realm of supernatural focus. Both resolutions of the problem contain "mysteries," but Hemingway's mysteries are humanistic rather than theological.

Hemingway's consistent belief in the freedom of the individual to make responsible choices was paid for at the painful expense of having constantly to wage battle with the fearful unpredictability of the future. If man is really free in the isolated moment of time, the importance of what he does and does not do in that moment are staggering. He has in effect elected to create the universe all by himself, and he has made himself answerable for the worth of his creation. Standing apart from the flux of sensations which eternally succeed themselves, he becomes the sole maker of time and meaning. He asserts his freedom not only from the guides of tradition, but also from his total experience of the past—from all the selves that he was in other existences. For, to create the new moment of time, he must create himself whole and unique in that moment; and this means that he must destroy what he was before that moment.

A constant act of creative will and a constant sense of universal responsibility conjoin in the awareness of the Hemingway hero. And the omnipresent threat which hands over his head is *nada*—a total whimsical destruction to his will, his responsibility, and the *meaning* which he has paid so highly for. The code is the tentative bridge which he erects into the future to effect a passage over the shadow; it is a network of promises to himself of what the future is likely to bring in the way of challenges and how he will respond to those challenges. It is tentative, flexible, and subject to swift changes; but, according to his capacity to redeem those promises to himself which can be kept, it gives the Hemingway hero that minimum amount of surety and rest in a quixotic world which is his only guide to the future.

Let us continue with the bridge-metaphor just a little longer. If one support for the bridge is flung into the future, the other support goes back into the past. One end of the bridge's span depends on the capacity of man to make promises to himself; the other, on his capacity to forgive himself his mistakes and inadequacies. The importance of this rear support, forgiveness, is too easily underestimated. If a man is unable to forgive his past actions, he becomes insidiously but irrevocably determined by them; and he loses his freedom to make a new beginning. He loses contact with the immediate moment of time because he must forever be caught up in that old played-out moment of time. His forgiveness frees him from the past and makes it possible for him to project new promises into the future, but it does not allow him to wipe out the past: "No, himself said. You have no right to forget anything. You have no right to shut your eyes to any of it nor any right to forget any of it nor to soften it nor to change it." Forgiving without forgetting is a large order for the human species, but projected promises without out a tough fibrous memory to give them substance would mean an inevitable descent into the chaos of the shadow.

Now let us return to "A Clean Well-Lighted Place" to see if we can find corroboration for some of these notions about the code. The story, it seems to me, can be read as a metaphor of the code. The clean and pleasant café is a lighted island within the darkness and confusion of the city. It is a place where those without the illusions of belief (religion, youth, confidence, family ties, insensitive indifference) can come, can sit, can drink with dignity; can find a small surcease or point of rest from their constant awareness of the meaninglessness of life and their struggles to oppose that meaninglessness. The story makes a spatial image for the code, which is, of course, a temporal metaphor, not a spatial one; but its quick focus on the old man suggests a temporal dimension as well. He had attempted to commit suicide the week before because "he was in despair." When asked what he was in despair about, one of the waiters answers "Nothing." We have already noticed how many of Hemingway's tyro-figures are in constant fear of this same "nothing," which keeps them from going to bed at night without a light on, which makes them eager to find the opiates of the radio, whiskey, or immersion in work or sex, which Mr. Frazer chronicles in "The Gambler, the Nun, and the Radio."

But having tried to kill himself out of despair, the old man comes to the café to rest momentarily from his fight. Hemingway takes special care to point up his dignity. The older waiter defends the old man from the younger waiter: "This old man is clean. He drinks without spilling. Even now, drunk. Look at him." And when he leaves the café he is described as "walking unsteadily but with dignity." The word "dignity" is the key to the operation of the code. In the creative act of imposing meaning on a senseless universe, in making the passage across the shadow, the Hemingway hero who works within the code may achieve *dignity* as the sole value for the game he has played. We have seen that the Major in "In Another Country" possessed it; that Santiago possessed it; that even Harry ("The Snows of Kilimanjaro") and Francis Macomber gained it in their deaths. We saw that almost the total lesson of Frederick Henry's experiences in *A Farewell to Arms* was directed toward making him responsible for his *self* in order that he could achieve dignity and some sombre meaning out of Catherine's death. The clean well-lighted place is the structure that man imposes on the chaos to wrest order and temporal regularity out of a meaningless flux of sensations. But this structure is not equal to the chaos it opposes. The café must close eventually, and its customers must leave again to face the nothingness which leads to despair. And even when it is open, the leaves of the trees throw shadows into the café; the nothingness can invade and disrupt the imposed order at any time.

It is interesting to notice how frequently Hemingway has explicitly and implicitly used the image of "the clean well-lighted place" as the arena of conflict, the dramatic locus of an onslaught or a challenge. The lighted lunchroom into which the two gunmen enter bringing machined and absurd terror in "The Killers" is such a place. The fire in the hobo jungle near the railway embankment in "The Battler" where Nick meets the punchdrunk fighter and his Negro friend is such a place. The cone of light that floods the prize ring in "Fifty Grand" is the same place. And the lighted sands in the middle of the darkened plaza where Manuel receives his *cogida* in "The Undefeated" is that same place. We could add the bull rings of *Death in the Afternoon,* the glow of the campfire in "The Snows of Kilimanjaro" into which the hyena and death will creep, or the operating table under the white lights of *A Farewell to Arms.* In each case, the clean well-lighted place is a temporary stay against confusion and terror. But when the terror remains on the outside, it is "the good place" of "Big Two-Hearted River," or the unbelievably white crown of Kilimanjaro, or the shining sands where the yellow lions play in Santiago's dreams. The clean well-lighted place is thus both an image of the code and a hopeful dream of its transcendent reality.

In this context the apparent hedonism of Hemingway's professed morality takes on a different coloration. In *Death in the Afternoon* he wrote: "So far, about morals, I know only that what is moral is what you feel good after and what is immoral is what you feel bad after and judged by these moral standards, which I do not defend, the bullfight is very moral to me because I feel very fine while it is going on . . . and after it is over I feel very sad but very fine" (4).

His characters—amazingly guiltless for twentieth-century literary characters—have similar emotional standards of morality. Catherine Barkley wishes she could do something that was really sinful; Harry Morgan is described thus after he machine-guns the four Cubans: "All the cold was gone from around his heart now and he had the old hollow, singing feeling and he crouched low down and felt under the square, wood-crated gas tank for another clip to put in the gun."

Jake Barnes feels rotten after he arranges Brett's liaison with Pedro Romero and Brett gives the classic formulation of the moral code: "You know it makes one feel rather good deciding not to be a bitch." We must investigate the relation of this emotional test of morality to the code which is its justification. I think we will find that it is neither so haphazard nor so untraditional a system of determining "rights" and "wrongs" as it originally appeared to the readers and critics of the early 1930's.

Since the code is designed to function in the place of absolute and externally imposed guides on human conduct, the delegation of the judgment of behavior will inevitably be given to the involuntary emotions. We have already noticed the consistent anti-intellectualistic bias of Hemingway's perspective (a bias which in this, as well as in other aspects of his work, makes him a twentieth-century heir to his Transcendental grand-uncles), and it would be strange for him to deny the primacy of the feelings in this most subjective area. Hemingway has persistently argued that values are a product and not a determinant of experience: ". . . when they have learned to appreciate values through experience, what they seek is honesty and true, not tricked, emotion. . . ." Hence, it would follow—as in any other variation of a pragmatic code—that "goods" and "bads" can only be ascertained after the process has come to some sort of completion. The "good" is not, in Hemingway, that which man wants to do; it is that which gives man a feeling of self-completion ("wholeness") after he has done it; and this sense of pleasure may be achieved through indulgence of one's whims or sometimes through the sacrifice of immediate desires.

Further, Hemingway makes a distinction between the people who can be trusted in their self-trust and those that cannot. One of his constant and frequently irritating strategies is to divide the human race into those who are qualified to live by the rigors of the code (those who are "one of us") and the others who are too flabby in their self-indulgence, too susceptible to a variety of illusions concerning themselves and life to be allowed to take over the responsibilities of creating their own lives. We will examine this as a dramatic theme in *The Sun Also Rises* in a later chapter, but there is hardly a Hemingway fiction which does not make its arbitrary division between those possessing what Emerson called "an active soul" and those others who are mere "formalists" in living. The fictitious organization of *Across the River and Into the Trees, El Ordine Militar, Nobile y Espirituoso de los Caballeros de Brusadelli,* is perhaps the most notorious example in his fiction of the willful line which Hemingway frequently drew between the "in's" and the "out's" (the professionals and the tourists). And his basis of inclusion is perhaps overly arrogant, but it is not without a guiding principle:

> I wish he did not have to have that glass eye, the Colonel thought. He only loved people, he thought, who had fought or been mutilated.
> Other people were fine and you liked them and were good friends; but you only felt true tenderness and love for those who had been there and received the castigation that everyone receives who goes there long enough.
> So I'm a sucker for crips, he thought. . . . And any son of a bitch who has been hit solidly, as every man will be if he stays, then I love him (71).

The same distinction is arbitrarily made in *To Have and Have Not* where the title—ambiguous as most of Hemingway's titles are—underscores the distinction. Those who "have" wealth, security, position, and the protective comforts which these possessions erect as a barrier against the elemental struggle of life, are also those who "have not" been there; hence they have no basic experience from which to create meaningful values. That Hemingway consistently ignored or underrated the equally real struggle which may take place under the camouflage of "respectability" and social forms is perhaps a regrettable indication of his lack of empathy and the narrowness of his fictional range; but it should not keep us from seeing that his test of inclusion rests on a solid pragmatic base. Those "who had been there" and had survived had been taught the implacable rules of the game on their heart and pulse beats; they cannot countenance the illusions of the "out's," because their knowledge of the stakes involved forces them to accept the reality of life as a grim, relentless struggle. "Only so much do I know, as I have lived," said Emerson; and, if he was more optimistic in his hope that all men could learn to become defiant and self-reliant than Hemingway was, still the intuitive bases of their faiths are similar and equally responsible.

From this viewpoint Hemingway's concern with the "techniques" of professionalism may also take on a different cast.[4] "Only so much do I know, as I have lived," makes a constant active quest for experience a fundamental prerequisite for knowledge. The soul which would become alive must be as fully exposed or receptive to life as possible; the preferential emphasis on *doing* proceeds from the pre-Deweyan faith that it is *doing* which leads to *being* and not the reverse. Hemingway's passion for knowing how things are done and what it feels like to do them—manifested in his private life as well as in his fictions—need not be labored here. From the mechanisms of making love in a Venetian gondola to the experience of walking through the working-class district of Milan to a hospital, Hemingway has taken on the gargantuan task of recording in his fictions almost everything he has patiently and obsessively learned.

Characteristically, as we saw in "Big Two-Hearted River," he will mercilessly analyze a process of action into its slowmotion components. At times the effect is merely silly or exclusively "knowing" as when Colonel Cantwell "reaches accurately and well" for a fresh bottle of Valpolicella. This insatiable desire to be expert in all areas of life can lead undeniably to a kind of grotesque over-concern with and over-valuation of the trivial (as when we are meant to admire Robert Jordan's professional knowledge of horses or Professor MacWalsey's expert knowledge in handling himself in tough saloons); but it also acts to maintain an ever-vigilant alertness and open receptivity to the challenges of every moment. It insures a kind of "activity" of the soul, or at least a forced physical awareness to the offerings of the "Daughters of Time, the hypocritic Days," which may decrease the threshold degree of resistance to new experience. And finally, the concern with the techniques of action gives the hero a program of behavior within which he may make a positive confrontation of the new moment where the mechanisms of his learned responses may aid him in successfully bridging the shadow of the passage and creating an order where none existed before.

III

We may not leave this discussion of the Hemingway code, however, without making a provisional attempt to deal with two strong criticisms that have frequently been levied against it. One persistent attack would deny the code of any philosophic substance on the grounds that Hemingway's heroes are either adolescents or mindless automata and hence their behavior is of the passing interest to a reader that a travelling freak show may engender. The other line of attack, closely related to the first, takes various forms and is rarely as explicit as in my descriptions; however, it can be summed up as a simple denial of Hemingway's relevance because of the inadequacy of his world view. He just does not possess a mature enough vision of evil to come to serious grips with the problems of the modern human condition.

I suppose that the simplest way of defending Hemingway, or any other artist, against attacks of such a nature is to deny the pertinence of the criticism. The artist is under obligation only to create mimetic worlds which may engage the imaginations of his audience; his psychological or philosophical competence is immaterial unless it seriously detracts from the successful workings of his art. "Let those who want to save the world. . . ." said Hemingway; and the creation of a philosophical formula which will resolve the agonizing ambiguities of our modern uncertainties is surely a strategy for saving the world. However, inasmuch as these criticisms are directed ostensibly at the successful workings of Hemingway's art, it would be dishonest criticism on my part to ignore their existence.

And since the two attacks are really extensions of one another, I shall somewhat Procrusteanly combine them for economy's sake in some excerpts from D. S. Savage's withering analysis of Hemingway's work:[5]

> His typical central character, his "I," may be described generally as a bare consciousness stripped to the human minimum, impassively recording the objective data of experience. He has no contact with ideas, no visible emotions, no hopes for the future, and no memory. He is, as far as it is possible to be so, a *de-personalized* being.

> The Hemingway character is a creature without religion, morality, politics, culture or history—without any of those aspects, that is to say, of the distinctively human existence.

> The characters of Hemingway reflect accurately the consciousness of the depersonalized modern man of the totalitarian era, from whom all inward sources have been withdrawn, who has become alienated from his experience and objectivized into his environment.

Some of Mr. Savage's strictures we have, I think, already dealt with; the more important ones we can try to counter. We saw that the operation of the code depends on precisely those "inward sources" which are denied existence. The code is created largely because the Hemingway hero is unwilling to accept the fatality of the coming moment; it is his un-illusioned hopes for the future which cause him to act at all, rather than to take the much easier way of reacting passively to circumstances: "It is silly not to hope, he [Santiago] thought. Besides I believe it is a sin." And we also saw that the Hemingway heroes are not "men without memories," but men who are determined not to become slaves to their pasts (memories); they are men who have made signal attempts to become masters of the present; and they know that they can strive to do this only through disengaging the present moment from all past moments. It is this, as we saw, that makes the act of self-forgiveness so important in the building of the code.

We can evidence this through one of the discussions in *For Whom the Bell Tolls* where Anselmo and Jordan talk about the need of killing in war. Anselmo says:

"I am against all killing of men."
"Yet you have killed."
"Yes. And will again. But if I live later, I will try to live in such a way, doing no harm to anyone, that it will be forgiven."
"By whom?"
"Who knows? Since we do not have God here any more, neither His Son nor the Holy Ghost, who forgives? I do not know."
"You have not God any more?"
"No. Man. Certainly not. If there were God, never would He have permitted what I have seen with my eyes. . . . I miss Him, having been brought up in religion. But now a man must be responsible to himself."
"Then it is thyself who will forgive thee for killing."
"I believe so," Anselmo said. "Since you put it clearly in that way I believe that must be it. But with or without God, I think it is a sin to kill" (41).

It would seem to me that it is anything but a *de-personalized* man who is willing to take on his own conscience the sole responsibility for his acts; and it is anything but "a bare consciousness stripped to the human minimum" that would have the odd combination of humility and pride to enable him to forgive himself his sins. It may be, from a philosophical point of view, that Hemingway's image of man gives entirely too much credit for the workings of a principle of divinity within

that man; but this is precisely opposite to Mr. Savage's denunciation. His other claims—that the Hemingway hero has "no visible
emotions" and "has become alienated from his experience"—I
believe we have already dealt with. It seems to me that this
general argument is based on the fallacy of construing the
sportsman's code to be the Hemingway code. I hope we have
shown that this is not the case.

It is probably true, on the other hand, that Hemingway does
lack a fashionable sense of evil, which is often considered today
to be a "mature" world view. Offhand I can think of no Hemingway character who is an animation of Original Sin; I can
think of no action in a Hemingway plot which could aptly be
described as one of motiveless malignity. There are many instances of evil, or certainly unpleasant, happenings in Hemingway's fiction, and most of his characters would patently fail
to qualify for sainthood; but evil as such does not play an important role in his work. And because there is this uncommon
deficiency, there is also a lack of concern with a torturing sense
of guilt or a crazed need for redemption. This may explain why
attempts to explicate his work in terms of Christological symbolism rarely prove illuminating in any way. And here, too, we
may find a precedent in Emerson—himself very unfashionable
in his indifference to evil. His famous exhortative approach to
evil could almost be synonymous with what seems to have been
Hemingway's: "Good is positive. Evil is merely privative, not
absolute: it is like cold, which is the privation of heat. All evil
is so much death or nonentity."

This citation returns us to what we have seen as one of Hemingway's major concerns: the emotional paralysis of man faced
with the overwhelming envelopment of *nada,* of "nonentity,"
and his resolute determination to impose meaning on that which
is without meaning. Had he come to believe that this struggle
was fruitless, he might have converted his vision of privative
emptiness into positive evil. His faith in man (and, I suppose,
in himself) would not allow him to do this. It may be that
this faith was an inordinate one, but such a question is surely
beyond the jurisdiction of literary criticism. It is certain that his
faith allowed him to project an image of man-as-hero which is
unparalleled in twentieth-century writing. This, it would seem
to me, indicates a strength and not a deficiency.

Jean-Paul Sartre, in a passage which has the dubious distinction of being unfair to both Hemingway and Albert Camus,

writes: "When Hemingway writes his short, disjointed sentences, he is only obeying his temperament. He writes what he sees. But when Camus uses Hemingway's technique, he is conscious and deliberate, because it seems to him upon reflection the best way to express his philosophical experience of the absurdity of the world."[6] Leaving the question of Sartre's judgment of Camus's purposes aside, I find it very strange that the distinguished French existentialist should decide out-of-hand that the one novelist writes on the basis of deliberate reflection and the other, seemingly, without thinking at all.

It makes an interesting hypothesis to think of Hemingway as a compulsive, automatic writer, "obeying his temperament" like a lemming racing to the sea; but it is less an act of responsible literary criticism than another instance of the deeply rooted European tradition which is determined to regard American literature as the casual off-droppings of noble or ignoble savages. The difficulty, as has so frequently been the case in the judgments of other major American writers by both native and foreign critics, is the stubborn refusal to recognize that American literature has always been marked by a powerful commitment to an overriding moral purpose. Literature in an open democratic society must do more than entertain and instruct; it must also function as a potential instrument for the creation of identity and of culture definition. Emerson's "liberating god" offers the metaphors of his vision to his society in order that its individuals may become *themselves* in their creative participation in those metaphors. The tropes of the "god" are fluid incitements toward *becoming,* not dogmatic pronouncements of *being.* It would not be too much to say, in Whitman's phrase, that the function of the American writer is "to be commensurate with a people"; and a people, at that, characterized throughout its history by metamorphosis, not stasis.

Because of this overriding function, consciously or unconsciously accepted by every major American writer, the individual works of American literature are curiously "open" on at least one end. Through a variety of experimental devices in style, structure, symbolism, and through the use of *personae,* the reader is invited—sometimes forced—to "live into" the work, to create his own values out of the collision of his experience and that which the successful work plunges him into. We have noticed that Hemingway's style, his use of the tyro protagonist, and his characteristic structures are shaped to this end of implicating a reader in the rhythms of growth which inform his fictions; and we noticed as well that the climax of the implication (in his best fictions) occurs with an act of self-discovery or self-revelation. Melville's "shock of recognition" or James's "suddenly determined absolute of perception" are examples of the same immediacy which is the bardic aim of American literature.

However, no writer can possibly be "commensurate with a people," particularly with a people as heterogeneous and purposely committed to change as has been the American people. The writer is consequently led to a kind of personal "invisibility," so that his actual personality will not impede the process of reader participation. The reader will be presented with narrator-protagonists (frequently unformed adolescents like Nick Adams) or with abstracted personages devoid of social reality but charged with mythic or symbolic attraction. There will thus be a very strong ironic distance between the actual flesh-and-blood writer (in almost no case in American literature do we really know who *he* is) and the pose or series of poses which the writer projects into his fictions and sometimes into public life.

To overlook this ironic distance is to fall into the trap of equating the man with the writer's mask—to assume, as Sartre does, that Hemingway lacks some essential intelligence or minimal self-consciousness, and that he cannot possibly be standing apart from his creations paring his fingernails or oiling his shotgun with casual insouciance. I would suggest that Hemingway's writing-mask can be sketchily characterized as a curious synthesis of some of the elements of Mark Twain's mask and Walt Whitman's mask, with certain added embellishments of his own. All three writers seemed to enjoy the role of the knowing innocent abroad, and all three seemed to enjoy "playing the fool" on occasion, as well as being the butt of their own jokes. None of them considered himself above that kind of sly defensive humor which allowed two modern American Nobel Prize winners to describe themselves as "just a country boy" and Ole Possum. But to equate Mark Twain with Huck Finn and to forget the shrewd man standing ironically *behind* Huck Finn, or to dispose of Whitman as the sounder of "the barbaric yawp" would be a strange aberration for a literary critic to indulge in. And yet this aberration has been literally endemic among Hemingway critics.

I have tried to demonstrate not the validity but the presence of a sound philosophical base for the Hemingway code. If we can assume that Albert Camus's attempt to present an expression of, and an artistic resolution to, "the philosophical experience of the absurdity of the world" is a product of removed reflection and considered design—then we must grace Hemingway with the same prerogatives of the non-automatic writer. To do otherwise would surely lead us into very non-Sartrean effusions on divine inspiration and shamanism.

CHAPTER 6

Of Time and Style

I

DURING the Caporetto retreat in *A Farewell to Arms,* one of the engineering sergeants steals a clock from an abandoned house, and Frederick Henry forces him to return it. The incident is thoroughly trivial except as it makes a small preparation for Henry's later antagonism to the sergeant, but I should like to suggest a further significance which was probably not intended. The idea of hauling a clock along in the chaotic confusion of a mass retreat is deliciously grotesque enough to characterize the sergeant, but it also can serve as an emblematic indication of Hemingway's contemptuous unconcern with the conventions of horological time. Nor should this be surprising in terms of our discussion in the last chapter of the operation of the Hemingway code. Only two kinds of time enter into Hemingway's fiction in any significant way; these are that time which we may call "geological"—the time that is used to measure the erosion of continents and the shrinking of mountains; and the *now*—that time which has been variously described as "the moment of truth," "the captive now," or "the perpetual now."[1] In different ways these two concepts of time conspire to aid in the formation of Hemingway's style, his aesthetic, and the characteristic concerns and directions of his fiction. Although we have implicitly alluded to this aspect of his work in other places, we may now try to discover its inner workings and to estimate the importance of its function in terms of Hemingway's over-all fictional approach. Having done this, we will then examine *For Whom the Bell Tolls* to test out and to illustrate our findings.

In *Green Hills of Africa* we find what must be the longest and most rhythmically flowing sentence in all of Hemingway's work.

I shall only quote it in part, but it is even a good deal longer than the following:

> That something I cannot yet define completely but the feeling comes when you write well and truly of something and know impersonally you have written in that way . . . and when, on the sea, you are alone with it and know that this Gulf Stream you are living with, knowing, learning about, and loving, has moved, as it moves, since before man, and that it has gone by the shoreline of that long, beautiful, unhappy island since before Columbus sighted it and that the things you find out about it, and those that have always lived in it are permanent and of value because that stream will flow, as it has flowed, after the Indians, after the Spaniards, after the British, after the Americans and after all the Cubans . . . are all gone as the high-piled scow of garbage, bright-colored, white-flecked, ill-smelling, now tilted on its side, spills off its load into the blue water, turning it a pale green to a depth of four or five fathoms as the load spreads across the surface, the sinkable part going down . . . ; the stream, with no visible flow, takes five loads of this a day . . . and in ten miles along the coast it is as clear and blue and unimpressed as it was ever before the tug hauled out the scow; and the palm fronds of our victories, the worn light bulbs of our discoveries and the empty condoms of our great loves float with no significance against one single, lasting thing –the stream (148-50).

This passage illustrates imperceptibly flowing geological time with a romantic vengeance; and, although Hemingway's thinking is not usually so explicitly directed to the view, *sub specie aeternitatis*, as we see here, this concept of time is rarely completely absent from his notions on life and art. He chose the title for *The Sun Also Rises*, his first major novel, from those passages in Chapter I of Ecclesiastes which closely parallel the above, and these same passages were read at his burial service. In his fiction he used images of mountains and the sea and natural countryscapes (as well as the rain in *A Farewell to Arms*) to reflect this long view of time which comments ironically on the vanity of human intercourse played against a sonorous background: "One generation passeth away, and another generation cometh: but the earth abideth for ever." Santiago's battle with the fish takes place on that same inexorably moving stream, and Harry Morgan bleeds his life into it. Richard Cantwell moves among the well-worn stones of a city notorious for its long tradition of vanities, and he dies fittingly across the river and almost into the trees. And Robert Jordan's love and death are framed by the rugged Spanish mountains which are not unlike the towering peak of Kilimanjaro.

"What profit hath a man of all his labour which he taketh under the sun?" To this unanswerable question Hemingway seemed to find a meaningful response in the fact that "the earth abideth for ever," and "the things you find out about it . . . are permanent and of value," even though knowledge and all the records that men leave will also succumb to extinction in the slow erosion of time. We noticed in the last chapter that the image of "a clean well-lighted place" could sometimes become an image of a transcendent reality in which the transiency and ephemerality of human existence were suddenly locked in another dimension of time; that feeling, in other words, which Hemingway could not yet define completely arcs itself out of human time and becomes one and immortal with the earth that abideth forever.

Hemingway's metaphysic of time, then, will be an attempt to squeeze the moment into that distilled, charged essence of felt emotion which, as we have seen, gave him a feeling of immortality. And in order to portray this essentially mystical experience in a prose narrative (which takes place in terms of straight sequential time), Hemingway will experiment with language and portrayal of action in an effort to simulate *contraction* and *expansion* of events simultaneously. An early indication of the direction that his prose will seek may be seen in the description of the bullfighter Maera's death in one of the miniatures of *in our time*: "There was a great shouting going' on in the grandstand overhead. Maera felt everything getting larger and larger and then smaller and smaller. Then it got larger and larger and larger and then smaller and smaller. Then everything commenced to run faster and faster as when they speed up a cinematograph film. Then he was dead."

The device, very crude here, is effective only because of the movement of the narrator into Maera's point of view, and then his shockingly abrupt removal in the final sentence. But the careful regulation of tempo in the passage—the accelerating pace of the words themselves (short simple words connected by temporal conjunctions forced into motion through the rhythmic repetition)—presages the much more sophisticated uses of this device which Hemingway will later employ. The

ironic contrasting staccato of the last sentence—now a commonplace technique in modern prose—stops the action like a bullet
and shifts the narrative point of view outside of the human
context to something that is almost like the long impersonal
view of the ever-abiding earth.

Some three years later (1927), Hemingway's mastery of this
stylistic device had developed immeasurably, as we can see in
the opening paragraph of "In Another Country," where there
is no residuum of dramatic action to force the alternate closings
and openings of time: "In the fall the war /was always there,
but we did not go to it any more. It was cold in the fall in Milan
and the dark came very early. Then the electric lights came on,
and it was pleasant along the streets looking in the windows.
There was much game hanging outside the shops, and the snow
powdered in the fur of the foxes and the wind blew their tails.
The deer hung stiff and heavy and empty, and small birds blew
in the wind and the wind turned their feathers. It was a cold
fall and the wind came down from the mountains."

This is really a passage of extraordinary stylistic subtlety
which analysis can hardly plumb, but perhaps we can indicate
some superficial procedures which have a bearing on this problem
of time. The time sense of the passage could be described as
"suspended present," even though the narrator is recounting
the events from a point in the future looking back into the past.
Throughout the story we are aware that this has already
happened, that this is being told to us through the processes
of selective remembrance. And yet the descriptions are rendered
with an overpowering sense of immediacy as though they *had
happened, but had not yet ceased to happen.* The effect is to
isolate this segment of artificially circumscribed time in its
natural momentum and to pluck it out of the meaningless tick-
ing of sequential time. Hemingway in effect has returned the
clock to the abandoned house and imposed his own time sense
on the events he has chosen to chronicle.

A closer examination of the passage will at least indicate the
control which Hemingway has achieved in manipulating his
effects. The speech rhythms in the excerpt clearly echo the
rhythms of the King James Version in their sonority and
finality of phrasing. This effect is largely a result of the
deliberate repetition of words and sentence structure; the poetic
connotations of the recurrent "and's" and the auxiliary "was,"
which becomes almost an active verb of *existence* instead of a

mere connective; and the pervasive hint of Elizabethan formality in the locutions ("but we did not go to it . . . ," ". . . and the dark came very early," "and the wind blew their tails," etc.). This effect is given additional support by the diction (short simple words, minimal use of adverbs, an almost ponderous emphasis on adjectives used not to modify but to bring into *being* as it were).

The imagery demonstrates how well Hemingway had learned the lesson of the unnoticed detail which stimulates emotion: "and the snow powdered in the fur of the foxes and the wind blew their tails. The deer hung stiff and heavy and empty, and small birds blew in the wind and the wind turned their feathers." This is highly impressionistic description; everything is seen in what is actually a very abstracted, non-concrete selection of detail, and yet it gives the illusion of being extremely realistic. As we noticed in our discussion in Chapter II of one of the miniatures, the realism is not in what is seen, but in the incontrovertible fact that someone is intensely *seeing*; and in line with this discussion on the uses of time, that act of seeing is so intense as to become identified in its abstractness with the way the mountains themselves might see such a scene. The cumulative roll of the passage persuades the reader that this is the way it was, and thus has it always been, and thus will it ever be. The small birds will always blow in the wind, and the wind will always turn their feathers.

And the references to the stability of the seasons, the weather, the wind and the mountains suggest an implicit awareness of the long Ecclesiastes view of time. Although Hemingway introduces the word "always" only in the first sentence, and there ironically to describe a temporal, not an eternal event, the eternality of the "always" carries through the whole paragraph. And finally we must at least call attention to the hinted appearance of the "clean well-lighted place" image (". . . the electric lights came on, and it was pleasant along the streets . . .") which contrasts with the cold fall and the sharp wind coming down from the mountains to suggest a temporary stasis of fixed illumination within the unimaginable eternity of relentless geological time.

Stylistically the passage fuses the *now* and the *always* in the moment of illumination (of the electric lights and the intense act of abstracted perception which the narrator expresses) when both become synonymous. Action (that which occurs in the

temporal onrush of flux) becomes so intensive in the act of
seeing that it becomes a distillation of itself and merges with
the monumental passivity of eternal time. Conversely, the
passivity of eternality is made active in the motion of the wind
and, by association, with the motion of the weather, and with
the mountains. The suspended moment of vision (the *now*) is
surrounded by the time which will move forever: but, because
everything in the description of "the forever" is frozen *in motion*
(the snow *is* powdering, the wind *is* blowing, the deer *are*
hanging, etc.), the total effect is to give the moment of seized
time the immortality of *always* time.

Harry Levin has pointed out one of the effects of Hemingway's style which, in this context, functions to aid in this time-
seizure: "Hemingway keeps his writing on a linear plane. He
holds the purity of his line by moving in one direction, ignoring
sidetracks and avoiding structural complications. By presenting
a succession of images, each of which has its brief moment when
it commands the reader's undivided attention, he achieves his
special vividness and fluidity."[2] But this succession of individual
images, like the frames on a reel of motion-picture film, do more
than create an effect of "vividness and fluidity." They also work
to force the illusion of "time suspended," caught and held and
merged into that greater time. which is timelessness. And to
experience that feeling of fusion between the *now* and the *always*
is to have something which is "permanent and of value" for
Hemingway, and of sufficient "profit" for all the seemingly vain
labor which man must do under the sun.

However, the handling of time in fiction is as much a
structural as a stylistic problem; hence we must re-investigate
Hemingway's employment of structure in terms of this aspect of
his aesthetic ideals. But instead of analyzing one of his fictions
as an illustrative test, we may turn again to that handy primer
of composition, *Death in the Afternoon.* One of the obvious
reasons why the bullfight so fascinated Hemingway was the
congenial metaphysic of time that was inherent in its formal
structure. The *corrida* takes place *in time*, within sequential horological time; as a matter of fact, quite punctually and precisely
so—as García Lorca pointed out in his great elegy for Ignacio
Sanchez Mejias, *a las cinco de la tarde*—at five o'clock in the
afternoon. But although it takes place in sequential clock time,
there is a more important designed time imposed upon it which
has the effect of enclosing the actual clock time in a formal

net of suspension. Hemingway describes the formal structure of the bullfight as follows: "There are three acts to the fighting of each bull and they are called in Spanish *los tres tercios de la lidia,* or the three thirds of the combat. The first act, where the bull charges the picadors, is . . . the trial of the lances. . . . Act two is that of the bandilleras. . . . and the third and final division is the death" (96-97).

As formally organized as a classical tragedy, and yet as open to improvisation as the *commedia dell'arte* because of the unpredictable behavior of both man and bull, the *corrida* makes a perfect symbolic stage for the enactment of Hemingway's code within the specific compression and expansion of time which his metaphysic demanded. That he felt that there could be this fusion of the *now* and the *always* in a great bullfight we have already seen, but it bears re-illustrating:

> If the spectators know the matador is capable of executing a complete, consecutive series of passes with the muleta in which there will be valor, art, understanding and, above all, beauty and great emotion . . . they have the hope sooner or later of seeing the complete faena; the faena that takes a man out of himself and makes him feel immortal while it is proceeding, that gives him an ecstasy, that is, *while momentary, as profound as any religious ecstasy;* moving all the people in the ring together and increasing in emotional intensity as it proceeds, carrying the bullfighter with it, he playing on the crowd through the bull and being moved as it responds in *a growing ecstasy of ordered, formal, passionate, increasing disregard for death* that leaves you, when it is over . . . as empty, as changed and as sad as any major emotion will leave you (206-7, italics added).

Within a structure which has artificially suspended time, the bullfight (under its ideal conditions) may further compress the suspended time (the *now*) to a point of excruciating ecstasy which results in a feeling of immortality (*always*-time). Hence we may expect that the structures of Hemingway's fictions will move in a direction toward the formal closed design of the bullfight but with opportunity within the internal context for that fusion of *now* and *always* which was so important to him. We should find, in other words, that the structures of Hemingway's fiction are in some special way conducive to an establishment of that formal confrontation which we found imaged in the metaphor of "a clean well-lighted place."

In our discussion of Hemingway's typical structures in Chapter IV, we divided Hemingway's stories into tyro stories ("unexploded bombs"), tutor stories (exemplary fables), and tutor-tyro stories ("epistemological" romances). Remembering that these arbitrary categories are far from exclusive, we discovered two characteristics which seemed to be common to all three structures, although varied in their uses and effects. These were a distinctive use of irony as a narrative technique, and a common development to a climax which would conclude in an act of self-discovery or self-realization. In the tyro story the "irony of the unsaid" worked through a measured withholding of shock and through a cumulative build-up of tension, resulting ideally in the release of emotion which the reader receives in the revelation of the true concealed drama in the fiction. In the tutor story, the irony resided in the symbolic suggestiveness of the parable, generating a stronger and stronger suspicion that the fiction meant more than it actually said, which tension is also ideally released in the reader's discovery of hitherto hidden "truths." And finally, in the tutor-tyro story, the irony was inherent in the dramatic distance between the knowledge of the narrator-protagonist and that of the actor-protagonist, and the released emotion again comes ideally in the reader's perception of the knowledge which is never explicitly detailed in the narrative action. In the light of our discussion on Hemingway's metaphysic of time, these two characteristics—irony and revelation—of Hemingway's fiction should function to control his structures in a way that will make them susceptible to that fusion of *now*-time and *always*-time which was the aim of his aesthetic.

I think it is possible to argue that this is exactly what happens. The first effect of the irony is that of "distancing"; this effect can work in many different ways, but the result is a radical displacement of the fictional experience away from the reader and away from the fictional equivalent of horological time, which is the realistic portrayal of human behavior within a convincing socio-historical dimension. The complex images or eidolons of the fictions are "struck from the float forever held in solution" (Whitman) and detached from objective reality to become an experience for reflection rather than for empirical perception. Such an effect is inevitable in the contemplation of any artistic object, of course, but Hemingway's employment of irony tends to magnify the process of distancing to a greater extent than is possible under the conditions of non-ironic narration. Further, we should note here that his characteristic concern with the presentation of internal rather than external images (the fantasy-projections of his own consciousness) will be an additional contributing element to this process of artistic detachment. The net effect is to give the individual stories the semblance of closed pockets; that is, they are defined and delimited by their own internal activity. Or, to return to the immediate problem, their artistic isolation and self-enclosure provide a structural equivalent for suspended temporality. What the style effects in giving an illusion of stoppage to the narrational flow of language, the ironic structures parallel in suspending and in closing in the simulation of human behavior in time.

The characteristic of developing a climax in the structure through the device of discovery or revelation operates to allow a passage from the *now*-time of the suspended and enclosed moment to the *always*-time of eternality. Revelation or illumination can be understood as an experience of *Gestalt* perception in which all the disconnected fragments of experience (conscious and subliminal) cohere with a suddenness and completeness that is involuntary, compelling, and frequently termed "ecstatic." The experience has often been described in terms of mystical transport and transcendental elevation. Without arguing its psychological validity, this experience has traditionally been associated with the intense emotion that aesthetic contemplation is able to offer under unique and rare circumstances, and it is a fact of human experience that what people call "the moment of truth" (the "light bulbs of our discoveries") is felt to be out of space and out of time—and hence immortal. At any rate, the structural devices which lead a narrator-protagonist to self-discovery, while insidiously drawing the reader into a participative self-discovery of his own, would seem to facilitate the possibilities of rendering Hemingway's full metaphysic of time in his fictional forms. The irony surrounds and suspends the action similar to the way the *barrera* and the traditional stylized design of the *faena* suspend horological time; and the moments of revelation in the fictions transcend the action in the same way that the great series of *suertes* creates the ecstasy of deliverance. We may conclude, therefore, that Hemingway's characteristic style and structure are both functional to the making of that illusion of mergence between *now* and *always* that is of cardinal importance to his aesthetic.

An additional note should be added, however. Hemingway has possessed no monopoly on the employment of an ironic narrative perspective or on a passionate interest in achieving moments of illumination in his fiction. Many other writers, especially Americans, have been similarly concerned and rather equally successful. James's fiction, particularly that of his later period, uses a similar and more sophisticated kind of irony, and his prose structures are very consciously built to lead to the moment of self-confrontation—the moment of "the suddenly determined absolute of perception." Hence, in characterizing Hemingway's treatment of time, we must add to the function of style and structure the typical violent action of his subject matter. As in the *corrida*, there is almost always in Hemingway's fictions a manifest physical conflict between the protagonist and a brutal animation of physical nature. It is not always an animal or another violence-bearing human being; it can be a heart attack or the death of a beloved. But it will be the invasion of *nada* in physical form, and therefore it can be opposed by the code only through some sort of physical activity. Hemingway's moment of fused time will generally be symbolized in a physical act—an act of killing or being killed, an act of sexual union, or a reaction of extreme physical shock which leads indirectly to the discovery of a truth. This temperamental emphasis on the physical will inescapably impart the distinctive Hemingway "shape" to his emotional communication of timelessness.

And finally we should notice that although the exigencies of literary criticism require us to deal with such categories as style, structure, subject matter, and theme as though they were separate and different strategies or modes of attack for dealing with a common problem, such an analytical division is sheerly mechanical. From our discussion of the code and from our discussion of Hemingway's metaphysic of time, we should realize that on the level of engaged fictional experience, the abstractions with which we clumsily approach the thing in itself, dissolve and coalesce in our moments of real artistic perception. For me such a moment occurs in the composite radical metaphor of "A Clean Well-Lighted Place"—a moment in which the temporal image of the code and the spatial image of fused time become one. "It was all a nothing and a man was nothing too. It was only that and light was all it needed and a certain cleanness and order." Here the "place" becomes the encloser and suspender of time and action, tenuous and removed; the "cleanness" and the "order" become the deliberate regularities with which man attempts to confront the "nothingness" with dignity and resolution; and the "light" is the measure of his success in illuminating the shadow and finding those truths about himself and life which are permanent and of value, and which make him in that seized moment know as much of immortality as he can ever know.

II

For Whom the Bell Tolls is, as we noted earlier, Hemingway's most ambitious novel. It is almost two hundred thousand words long; it is set in the foreground of an international civil war which was rather more complicated in its alliances and divisions than most; and it attempts to suggest all those experiences Hemingway had felt with Spain (perhaps his favorite country) that, as he notes in the last chapter of *Death in the Afternoon,* he had been unable to include in that book. Hence the novel is many things: an attempt to present in depth a country and a people that he loved very much; an effort to deal honestly with a highly complex war made even more complex by the passionate ideologies which it inspired; and, beyond all these, a struggle to cast a personal metaphor of his unique vision of life. Given Hemingway's peculiar strengths and weaknesses as a novelist, it is inevitable that the novel should fall short of his ideals; the remarkable thing, however, is the extent to which it is successful even in those areas in which it fails. Although our examination of the novel will be occupied largely with its attempts to render the metaphysic of time with which we have been concerned, we must remember that this is only one aspect of *For Whom the Bell Tolls,* and that there are many other ways of approaching it.[3]

As many critics have pointed out, the structure of *For Whom the Bell Tolls* is circular; its center, which we are never allowed to be unaware of, is the steel bridge which spans the gorge "in solid-flung metal grace." From that center all the actions of the novel, dramatic and symbolic, radiate in widening concentric circles of meaning. The Loyalist offensive depends on the certainty that the bridge be exploded so that the road will be closed to the movement of Fascist reinforcements. Robert Jordan's sole reason for going behind the enemy lines is to blow up the bridge; like Santiago, his mission is what he was born for. The disruption of Pablo's guerrilla band is directly related to the significance of the bridge; and the extermination of El Sordo's band on the hilltop is indirectly related to it as well. By extension, the bridge becomes symbolically a pivotal center for the destiny of mankind: ". . . there is a bridge and that bridge can be the point on which the future of the human race can turn." The bridge then is the absolute point of confrontation, the proper meeting of which ought to justify the code and provide that contact with immortality which the metaphysic of fused time demands. For this fusion to be successful, the novel must create the illusion that time has been suspended, contracted down to an explosive point of *now*, and expanded endlessly into a communicated sense of *always*.

The technical problems facing Hemingway in this attempt were enormous. He had chosen to depict a group action rather than the struggle of one man; and, although the novel ultimately concerns itself with Robert Jordan, there are more than a dozen other characters who must be fit into the dramatic organization and be suitably disposed of. Further, since Hemingway consciously wanted Robert Jordan's action to be a representative one, he had to find means of relating both Jordan and his action to situations and events outside of the immediate dramatic compass of the novel. However, this aim makes for additional problems; for every time Hemingway departs from the immediate "thing of the bridge," in order to expand the meaning of the action, he runs into the danger of opening up his closed stage and destroying the suspension of time. And yet if he does not do this, Jordan's adventures with the bridge may appear simply eccentric—the isolated maneuvers of a super-hero behind the Fascist lines.

Thus, on the one hand, if the suspension of time is lost, the novel will be judged according to its realistic depiction of an actual historical event, and the actions of its characters may justly be expected to reflect sociological and political realities. If, on the other hand, the action is not in some way universalized, it can be justly categorized as a romantic adventure story bearing no significant relationship to the setting which is its locale. We have already seen that Hemingway's powers were not those ordinarily associated with the doctrines of realism, and we have also seen that the abstractions of ideology were not the materials which engaged his creativity. The obvious solution to his problems he chose—for whatever reason—to ignore; namely, to write a fable, an exemplary story like *The Old Man and the Sea* which would be both suspended in time and universalized. It is probable that he wanted too much to record the Spanish war directly, or that he was committed still to the use of a tyro rather than a tutor character; at any rate, his resolution of these problems was not completely successful (as we may judge by the criticism which was levied against the novel) since justifications for both criticisms do exist in the novel's structure. But the novel is astonishingly successful even with its failures, and it will be useful to investigate how Hemingway dealt with these technical problems in the pursuit of his aesthetic fusion of time.

Hemingway's first strategy in attempting to create an illusion of suspended time was to isolate the novel temporally and spatially. General Golz's orders for the blowing of the bridge are, to be sure, provisional but in the dramatic development of the novel, the three-day action from Jordan's appearance with Anselmo to his final stand with the machine gun is as stylized and formally closed as the three act bull-fight. Using a seventy-hour time scheme for the novel's events and making that seventy-hour schedule apparent to the reader, Hemingway gives the appearance of employing horological time, but he does so only to transform it into his own time. There are several direct references to this transformation of time in the novel, of which the following is fairly representative:

> Maybe that is my life and instead of it being threescore years and ten it is forty-eight hours or just threescore hours and ten or twelve rather. Twenty-four hours in a day would be three-score and twelve for the three full days.
>
> I suppose it is possible to live as full a life in seventy hours as in seventy years; granted that your life has been full up to the time that the seventy hours start and that you have reached a certain age (166).

Thus we are constantly reminded that this is not seventy clock hours of sequential time, but seventy hours scooped out of time with a quite arbitrary beginning and an end. Pilar's introduction of the omen which she reads in Jordan's hand supports this time isolation; it is not minutes and hours that are passing in the novel, but Jordan's life. That is, the seventy clock hours measure doom instead of time, and the movement of doom in fiction can only be presented as "suspended time."

And we ought to note also that Hemingway takes great pains to document the passing of the time in these seventy hours. The meal times are described in detail; the sleeping time during the two nights is presented in such a way that the reader cannot possibly miss it; and the changes in weather and light during the three days and within each day are carefully delineated. The appearance of fighter and bomber planes in the sky, as well as the troop of Fascist cavalry on the ground, functions as much to punctuate the passing time as to develop the plot. And Jordan even gives his watch to Anselmo when he sends him to record the troop movements on the bridge. For we must realize that, if Hemingway wishes to suspend time in order to compress it in the novel, he cannot allow its passage within the scooped-out suspension to go unnoticed. The reader must be made aware of the swift and regular movement of time within the sequence of frozen time. Otherwise there will be no time for him to fuse.

But even as the novel is isolated temporally, it is also isolated spatially. The plot device of having the action take place behind the enemy lines makes a very natural spatial demarcation. The action is placed, as it were, in another country—and one where the normal laws of human behavior do not apply. The guerrillas are by definition "irregulars," improvising their own expedients to structure a life lived outside of normal socially controlled habits and *mores*. The placing of sentries to guard this isolated space accentuates its fictional distance, as does the action of Andrés's difficulties in getting through the Loyalist lines to deliver his message to Golz. The placement of the bridge over a gorge between two mountains, the concealed remoteness of Pablo's cave, and the general impression that the reader receives of the entire locale of the action being cupped in by a jagged mountain range effectively encloses the "stage" of the novel in a manner parallel to the way the arbitrary segmenting of time closes off the "act" that will be played on that stage. Something of both effects can perhaps be seen—as well as a sense of the circularity of the enclosure—in a comparison of the opening lines of the novel with those that end it:

> He lay flat on the brown, pine-needled floor of the forest, his chin on his folded arms, and high overhead the wind blew in the tops of the pine trees. The mountainside sloped gently where he lay; but below it was steep and he could see the dark of the oiled road winding through the pass.

Then he rested as easily as he could with his two elbows in the pine needles and the muzzle of the submachinegun resting against the trunk of the pine tree. . . . Robert Jordan lay behind the tree, holding onto himself very carefully and delicately to keep his hands steady. He was waiting until the officer reached the sunlit place where the first trees of the pine forest joined the green slope of the meadow. He could feel his heart beating against the pine needle floor of the forest.

The two scenes are remarkably similar, both in Jordan's prone position of watching and in the general description of his surroundings. But, in the seventy hours between the first and the last scene, the pine needles have been covered with snow and also blood; and Jordan has loved and killed and is now ready to be killed. He is, at the end, where he was at the beginning; the arc of the circle is just at the point of completion. And what the circle is meant to circumscribe is his whole life.

Because of the fictional requirement that a lifetime be compressed into three days, Hemingway made a fuller dramatic use of the memory flashback and of the interior monologue in this novel than in any of his fictions. We know more about Robert Jordan's past and about his thinking processes than about those of any other Hemingway protagonist. This is still not very much, but the exclusions in this case are justified on structural principles. Typically the events that Jordan remembers or thinks about are directly or indirectly related to the thematic necessities of the novel. Thus he remembers saying good-bye to his father at a railway depot as a prelude to his good-bye to Maria; his recollections of his grandfather's Civil War experience suggest a vertical identification in time between his grandfather's war and the one he is in the·midst of. The reflections on his father's suicide are dramatically motivated by his own awareness of the pressures which oppose him and the necessity that he places upon himself of performing well. It is only in the reminiscences of Gaylord's and the somewhat over-protracted musings on Democracy and Communism that the tight structure tends to break. It seems to me that in much of this latter material Hemingway loses his distance between himself and his protagonist (a flaw which becomes a catastrophe in *Across the River and Into the Trees*); and the tenuous suspension of time and space is momentarily lost. The employment of the device, however, is almost mandatory; for if we are to believe that Jordan's life is squeezed into seventy hours, we must believe that he had a life before the first of these hours began.

Hemingway broadens his use of this device to include memory recitals and straight third-person narratives of what have sometimes been called the "set-pieces" in the novel. These include Pilar's description of the taking of the town from the Fascists, Maria's recollection of her parents' deaths and of her violation, and the description of El Sordo's stand on the hilltop. Each of these is unnecessary to the plot, and in the narration of each the actual dramatic momentum to the novel ceases. But the stoppage of linear time in these three cases is achieved without breaking distance and without losing the illusion of isolation. Each description, in a sense, broadens or elongates the time that has been caught and held in suspension; each constructs, as it were, a thicker density of time to be contracted and exploded at the bridge.

Simultaneously the suspension of space and time makes it possible for Hemingway to get the effect of *always*-time; the removal of the events and human actions makes a hiatus between the reader's normal sense of time and that of the novel, imparting to the latter a tinge of "mythic" or "make-believe" time. And this tendency is also strengthened by several devices. The recurrent references to gypsy and folk superstitions have an enduring quality quite harmonious to the long view of time. The stylized pidgin-Spanish dialogue with its "thee's" and "thou's" is purposely archaic in sound to reinforce the "long" time.[4] And the nature imagery which pervades the novel reflects ages of seasons in their relentless recurrence. In this passage, for example, Jordan is reacting to the snowstorm:

> In the snowstorm you came close to wild animals and they were not afraid. They travelled across country not knowing where they were and the deer stood sometimes in the lee of the cabin. In a snowstorm you rode up to a moose and he mistook your horse for another moose and trotted forward to meet you. In a snowstorm it always seemed, for a time, as though there were no enemies. In a snowstorm the wind could blow a gale; but it blew a white cleanness and the air was full of a driving whiteness and all things were changed and when the wind stopped there would be the stillness (182).

The style in this excerpt could easily be examined with results very similar to those we discovered in the opening paragraph of "In Another Country." There is a formal stylization, the same use of repetition and echoings from the King James Version, and the insistent coercion of the "always." Thus we can see that Hemingway has patterned this novel in such a way as to isolate it spatially and temporally, to cast vertical wells within the linear suspended time, and to arrange for a possibility of archaic or "eternal" identifications in his dialogue and in his nature descriptions.

Within this complex time-frame the plot is stripped to simplicity. Jordan arrives with his orders at Pablo's cave, makes his arrangements, falls in love with Maria, has a slight obstructional deterrence from Pablo, explodes the bridge on schedule, and prepares to die when his broken leg makes it impossible for him to escape. The simplicity of the plot helps the process of time fusion, for the action starts rather slowly and accelerates increasingly to the final scene in the novel. It is pushed relentlessly by the ominous fatality of the palm reading and by the necessity to carry out the orders on schedule. The appearance of the cavalry troop and Pablo's treachery quicken the suspense, as does the knowledge that the Fascists are preparing to meet the attack. The switching of scenes toward the end of the novel between Andrés, who is trying to get his message through to Golz, and the scenes at the guerrilla camp are strongly reminiscent of D. W. Griffith's film splicing in *Intolerance*, and they serve the same function of heightening suspense and of speeding up the action by making every moment significant. The total effect of the plot acceleration is to "cram" the action intensively; that is, to supersaturate the density of time within its enclosed and suspended space.

And finally Hemingway explodes this charged pocket of time through a system of subtle identifications in which the character Maria becomes symbolic of Jordan's self-realization, of the universal rightness of the cause for which Jordan is offering his life, of Spain, and, ultimately, of ever-enduring Nature itself. This is an enormous load of meaning to place on one cropped head, and it is probable that it is not completely successful. But Jordan's experiences can be communicated only through his relationship to some one or thing apart from himself, and his transcendent sexual union with Maria is the most likely opportunity for becoming an objective correlative for the time fusion that is desired. We can try to point out the processes of these identifications analytically; the judgment of their success can only be a subjective one.

The achievement of *now*-time that Jordan and Maria create in their lovemaking is suggested frequently in the novel, and perhaps nowhere more elaborately than in the following attempt to reproduce the sensations of a particularly fulfilling sexual union. Notice in this passage the purposeful discarding of horological time (the watch in the first sentence) and the suggestion of *Leitmotif* in Jordan's prone position in relation to the pine trees:

> Then they were together so that as the hand on the watch moved, unseen now, they knew that nothing could ever happen to the one that did not happen to the other, that no other thing could happen more than this; that this was all and always; this was what had been and now and whatever was to come. This, that they were not to have, they were having. They were having now and before and always and now and now and now. Oh, now, now, now, the only now, and above all now, and there is no other now but thou now and now is thy prophet. Now and forever now. Come now, now, for there is no now but now. Yes, now. Now, please now, only now, not anything else only this now, and where are you and where am I and where is the other one, and not why, not ever why, only this now; and on and always please then always now, always now, for now always one now; one only one, there is no other one but one now, one, going now, rising now, sailing now, leaving now, wheeling now, soaring now, away now, all the way now, all of all the way now; one and one is one, is one, is one, is one, is still one, is still one, is one descendingly, is one softly, is one longingly, is one kindly, is one happily, is one in goodness, is one to cherish, is one now on earth with elbows against the cut and slept-on branches of the pine tree with the smell of the pine boughs and the night; to earth conclusively now, and with the morning of the day to come (379).

With what seems to be an echoed influence from Joyce and Cummings, Hemingway attempts to do something in this passage similar to the older waiter's parody of the Lord's Prayer in "A Clean Well-Lighted Place." As the effect of the short story is to give tangibility or "somethingness" to the repeated "nothing" of the prayer, in the novel the words "now," "always," "one," and "is," should ideally merge into one composite symbol of mystical transport in which *all is now one and always.* Hemingway reinforces this purpose in Jordan's reflections immediately after this scene: "She said La Gloria. It has nothing to do with glory nor La Gloire that the French write and speak about. It is the thing that is in the Cante Hondo and in the Saetas. It is in Greco and in San Juan de la Cruz, of course, and in the others. I am no mystic, but to deny it is as ignorant as though you denied the telephone or that the earth revolves around the sun or that there are other planets than this" (380). My own feeling is that this is a good example of the impossibility of rendering experience *directly* in language (especially sexual experience); but Hemingway's purpose and partial fulfillment can hardly be gainsaid.

Maria is thus the vessel of Jordan's complete self-realization; in his mergence with her, he has achieved the immortality of becoming "other," of losing himself into something that is not himself. As he tells her in his final goodbye, "Thou art me now too. Thou art all there will be of me." But we must investigate more closely what Maria *is*; for if she is only a mortal Spanish girl who is almost nineteen, Jordan's "immortality" is still susceptible to the destruction of time. First, her past experience as an innocent victim of brutal oppression identifies her strongly with the cause to which Jordan has committed himself; and this identification is strengthened by the "healing" virtues of Jordan's love for her. She has been inhumanly broken by her experience; her past mitigates against any chance of new life; but the cause promises to wipe out century-old oppression that man may be given a new beginning. This theme of the new beginning is evident in Maria's acceptance of Pilar's folk wisdom: "Nothing is done to oneself that one does not accept and that if I loved some one it would take it away." Hence Jordan's death leaves the vitality of the cause for which he dies untouched and even more resolute after his death.

Second, the symbolic connotations of Maria's name are obvious enough identifications with both Spain and the Virgin to need no further explication. Third, and more interestingly, she is consistently identified with images of regenerative nature and of life. She is called "rabbit" as Jordan's pet-name for her; her cropped hair is imaged as a field of growing wheat; and, as Jordan holds her in his arms, she becomes purely and simply "life" to him: "But in the night he woke and held her tight as though she were all of life and it was being taken from him. He held her feeling she was all of life there was and it was true" (264).

But we must not overlook the fact that in losing his isolate self in Maria, Jordan gains eternal life beyond his insignificant mortality. He becomes the earth that abideth forever, sinking his spirit in its impassive contempt for human time:

> Robert Jordan lay behind the trunk of a pine tree on the slope of the hill above the road and the bridge and watched it become daylight. He loved this hour of the day always and now he watched it; feeling it gray within him, as though he were a part of the slow lightening that comes before the rising of the sun; when solid things darken and the lights that have shone in the night go yellow and then fade as the day comes. The pine trees below him were hard and clear now, their trunks solid and brown and the road was shiny with a wisp of mist over it. The dew had wet him and the forest floor was soft and he felt the give of the brown, dropped pine needles under his elbows (431).

And this mergence is given final authority in the experience of "the earth-moving" and in Hemingway's explicit statement of the theme several paragraphs before the novel ends: "Robert Jordan saw them there on the slope, close to him now, and below he saw the road and the bridge and the long lines of vehicles below it. He was completely integrated now and he took a good long look at everything. Then he looked up at the sky. There were big white clouds in it. He touched the palm of his hand against the pine needles where he lay and he touched the bark of the pine trunk that he lay behind" (471).

We suggested earlier that *For Whom The Bell Tolls* could almost be considered a pastoral idyl; it would be more accurate in the context of this discussion of time to call it a pastoral elegy—one strangely similar to Whitman's "When Lilacs Last in the Dooryard Bloom'd." Like that great poem, it envelops death and temporal violence in a transcendent serenity and harmony. And, like the poem also, eternal time and the seized moment of realization are merged and made one in the design of a poetic metaphor—profoundly evocative and cleanly humanistic.

It remains only to suggest how the time fusion is made to become identical with the operation of the code. We mentioned earlier that, just as the explosion of horological time must radiate from the focal center of the novel, the bridge, so the moment of confrontation must likewise be integrally connected with the bridge. And just as Maria is somewhat too slight to hold the burden of symbolic meaning which is placed on her, the bridge is not solidly enough fixed as the center of the novel to become a fully convincing "clean well-lighted place" in terms of the code. However, within its limitations it works extraordinarily well and the identifications almost occur. The major technique which Hemingway employs to this end is the futility of the attack and the abortive failure of the entire bridge-blowing operation. ". . . that bridge can be the point on which the future of the human race can turn." However, the Fascists have already moved their reinforcements up the road to counter the foreknown attack, and it matters very little whether the bridge is blown up or not. In concrete military terms, the bridge is no longer the point on which the future of the war, or the human race, can turn. The explosion of the bridge, with all the human waste that accompanies it, is an absurdly meaningless event within the desperate flow of a losing war. It represents, in a grim and even sardonic way, the intrusion of *nada* into the illusions and courage of the group that has banded together into a cohesive unit in order to destroy the bridge and create meaning.

But in non-military terms, that is, in poetic terms, the *nada* is heroically bridged; the confrontation does become a point on which the future of the human race can turn; for mankind does conquer the futility of non-meaning in its resolute bravery and achieved oneness. The individuals within the group have been forged into a whole; even Pablo has come to realize in his temporary treachery that "having done such a thing there is a loneliness that can not be borne." Each of them does not achieve that mystical integration which is Jordan's and which is his imposition of meaning on the shadow; but General Golz's words into the telephone can stand as an emblem for the way the composite guerrilla group, representing the ideals of the Cause, and beyond that the determination of humanity to live lives of courage and dignity, have fronted the encroachments of "nothingness": "No. *Rien à faire. Rien. Faut pas penser. Faut accepter. . . . Bon. Nous ferons notre petit possible.*"

CHAPTER 7

The Sun Also Rises:
An Essay in Applied Principles

DURING the course of this book, I have purposely avoided discussing *The Sun Also Rises* (1926), Hemingway's first, and perhaps most completely successful novel, preferring to discuss it in isolation from any thematic or technical concerns. It is, in many ways, an anomalous work in Hemingway's lifetime of publication: it is characteristic Hemingway; yet it is an uncharacteristic Hemingway fiction. It was written partly out of a disgust with the empty Bohemianism of "The Lost Generation," but it has served to make that Bohemianism eminently attractive to succeeding generations of readers. It was read originally as a *roman à cléf* in which the major (and some of the minor) characters could be identified by those with the inside knowledge; time has made some of these very characters secure, living fictional beings.

Hemingway has insisted that *The Sun Also Rises* is a tragedy and not a "hollow or bitter satire,"[1] but criticism has been slow to accept either of his definitions. In fact, although it seems to me that some of the best of Hemingway criticism has concerned itself with this novel,[2] there is a surprising lack of unanimity among critics on what would seem to be basic non-controversial issues. Critics have divided handsomely on determining where the moral center of the book rests; some have found it in Pedro Romero, some in Jake Barnes, and there have even been spirited defenses of Robert Cohn. There have been attempts to read the book as an elegy on the death of love, and others to show that the sun does rise out of the wasteland.

When good critics disagree so violently, we can assume that there must be much smoke and much fire also, and that the novel must rest on a special base of ambiguity. Therefore I offer my reading of *The Sun Also Rises* not as an act of settlement or final explanation; however, having concerned ourselves almost exclusively with the way Hemingway's art was formed and how it seems to work in special contexts, it will be salutary to see if we can apply some of these general principles to what is unanimously agreed to be one of his superior artistic productions.

The difficulties of interpreting *The Sun Also Rises* in a clear and relatively certain manner stem in the main from two factors: the use of a particularly opaque first-person narrator; and the fact of Jake's wound which has rendered him impotent, while leaving him normally responsive to sexual desire. The first factor results in the bewilderment a reader will have in trying to locate the norms of "truth" in the novel; that is, since the entire novel is related directly by Jake Barnes, the reader can never be sure how reliable Jake's observations and judgments are. He does not know to what extent he must look at Jake ironically and to what extent sympathetically. And Hemingway has artfully (or accidentally) failed to provide the reader with obvious hints or standards of measurement within the novel which will aid the reader in directing his point of view. Thus, if the reader accepts Jake's story as completely authoritative, he must accept as well Jake's friends and their empty reboundings from one Parisian cabaret to another, from France to Spain and back to France again. If he decides, on top of that, that Jake is Hemingway's sympathetic spokesman, he can only conclude that the "tragedy" of the novel is inherent in Jake's inability to join in the fun. Decisions that Jake is an unreliable narrator, or that he is meant to be unsympathetic will lead to equally absurd readings in an opposite direction. Obviously he must be *mostly* reliable and *mostly* sympathetic. We will try to thread the precarious line of his maneuverings.

The fact of the wound separates Jake from the action in a way that makes this novel very different from all Hemingway's longer fictions. Jake's impotency deprives him of a typical Hemingway love-relationship, and because of the *milieu* in which the novel is placed, it forces him to be a spectator rather than a participator in the events of the novel. He can react intensely, but his actions will necessarily be passive; they will be struggles to "hold on" and to accept rather than to shape circumstances by the force of his direct will. Thus the novel is composed largely of "what happens" to Jake and how he copes with these happenings over which he is denied any control. In a sense this places him in a constant psychological situation of having to accept the absurd meaninglessness of his fate and somehow wrest some meaning from it. Hemingway makes special reference to his "biblical name," Jacob. This may suggest that like his namesake, Jake must wrestle until daybreak with an angel that is a demon; but, unlike his namesake, the "blessing" that will reward his powers to endure will merely ensure the prolongation of the struggle.

Jake's most elaborate statement of his code occurs during the fiesta at Pamplona. It is also close enough to the Hemingway code that we have seen in operation to stand as the value center of the novel:

> I thought I had paid for everything. Not like the woman pays and pays and pays. No idea of retribution or punishment. Just exchange of values. You gave up something and got something else. Or you worked for something. You paid some way for everything that was any good. I paid my way into enough things that I liked, so that I had a good time. Either you paid by learning about them, or by experience, or by taking chances, or by money. Enjoying living was learning to get your money's worth and knowing when you had it. You could get your money's worth. The world was a good place to buy in. It seemed like a fine philosophy. In five years, I thought, it will seem just as silly as all the other fine philosophies I've had.
>
> Perhaps that wasn't true though. Perhaps as you went along you did learn something. I did not care what it was all about. All I wanted to know was how to live in it. Maybe if you found out how to live in it you learned from that what it was all about (153).

If we can accept this statement as being true for Jake, it should follow that the novel will be a recording of Jake's painful lessons in learning how to live in the world while getting his money's worth of enjoyment for the price that is exacted from him. We can then, at least as a point of departure, examine the story as an "epistemological" novel.

From this standpoint the novel contains one tutor, Count Mippipopolous, and one anti-tutor, Robert Cohn. The Count has presumably paid in full for his ability to enjoy his champagne, his chauffeur, and his expensive tastes in women (he offers Brett $10,000 to go to Biarritz with him). His somewhat incongruous arrow wounds testify to the fact that "he has been there" and has learned how to extract values from his experience. His role as model is pointed to in an early three-way conversation with Brett and Jake:

> "I told you he was one of us. Didn't I?" Brett turned to me. "I love you, count. You're a darling."
> "You make me very happy, my dear. But it isn't true."
> "Don't be an ass."
> "You see, Mr. Barnes, it is because I have lived very much that now I can enjoy everything so well. Don't you find it like that?"
> "Yes. Absolutely."
> "I know," said the count. "That is the secret. You must get to know the values."
> "Doesn't anything ever happen to your values?" Brett asked.
> "No. Not any more."
> "Never fall in love?"
> "Always," said the count. "I am always in love."
> "What does that do to your values?"
> "That, too, has got a place in my values."
> "You haven't any values. You're dead, that's all."
> "No, my dear. You're not right. I'm not dead at all" (63).

The Count is more or less in the position of the Major's ideal man ("In Another Country") who has found things that he cannot lose. He has stripped his stockpile of illusions to the barest minimum, transferring the capitalistic ethic of exchange values to the sphere of the emotions. But, as he corrects Brett, he is not "dead," nor are his emotional transactions mutely mechanical or sterile. His moral position can be compared to that of the gambler who is willing to bet beyond the law of percentages; who will extend and back his play with a calculated risk of losing because part of the gusto of living (to "enjoy everything so well") depends on the exhilaration of exposure. The "stuffed-animal" conversation between Bill Gorton and Jake which occurs shortly after the above scene reinforces this distinction. Bill drunkenly tries to persuade Jake to buy a stuffed dog:

> "Mean everything in the world to you after you bought it. Simple exchange of values. You give them money. They give you a stuffed dog."

"We'll get one on the way back."
"All right. Have it your own way. Road to hell paved with unbought stuffed dogs. Not my fault" (74).

And several pages later Jake introduces Bill as a "taxidermist." "That was in another country," Bill said. "And besides all the animals were dead."

Beneath the current of wisecracking (and the dialogue here, as well as in the Burguete scenes, shows Hemingway's superb mastery of sophisticated stage talk), the Count's philosophy is contrasted and given higher valuation. A graded hierarchy of exchange value is implicitly established; the Count insists on a fair exchange; he will pay, but he wants his animals to be "live" and not stuffed. And he has trained himself to be an unillusioned connoisseur in distinguishing between life and its varied imitations. Bill's adaptation of the code is on a lower level of enjoyment. The "road to hell is paved with unbought stuffed dogs." He has no illusions about what he is paying for; he knows that all the animals are dead, but he is willing to forgo the supreme risk of paying for "life," by pursuing the pleasures that he can momentarily extract in the meaningless excitement of his "stuffed animals." His drunken trip to Vienna and his general behavior in Paris are a prelude to Frederick Henry's furlough in *A Farewell to Arms,* because Bill's commitment to enjoyment does not include a real risk of himself. And his position is representative of most of the sophisticated carousers who find an adequate symbol for their desires in the San Fermin fiesta in Pamplona.

But there is also a lower level of gradation in the "exchange-value" metaphor. The road to hell can be traveled swiftly by those who buy stuffed animals, since this is a considered purchase of ultimate emptiness and non-meaning. But that same road, as Hemingway makes clear in his insertion of the scenes with Woolsey and Krum—or with the Dayton, Ohio, pilgrims—is also paved with *unbought* stuffed animals. To deny oneself the ephemeral pleasures, even though they are without meaning, without having a more substantial value to embrace is an even emptier behavior. There are degrees of *rigor mortis* in the death-in-life as we see in the following expertly understated conversation:

"Playing any tennis?" Woolsey asked.

"Well, no," said Krum. "I can't say I've played any this year. I've tried to get away, but Sundays it's always rained, and the courts are so damned crowded."

"The Englishmen all have Saturday off," Woolsey said.

"Lucky beggars," said Krum. "Well, I'll tell you. Some day I'm not going to be working for an agency. Then I'll have plenty of time to get out in the country."

"That's the thing to do. Live out in the country and have a little car" (37).

To use the terminology that we have hitherto employed, the Woolseys and the Krums are unknowing tourists in life, paying exorbitant prices for nothing; the Bill Gortons are professional tourists who pay without illusions for the nothingness that they are willing to settle for; and the Count is the non-tourist professional who is determined to get his money's worth at the expense of exposing himself in the imposition of meaning on his emotional purchases.

This hierarchy of values is highlighted by the presence of the anti-tutor, Robert Cohn, who has the unfortunate burden of being "the horrible example" of the novel. He is Jake Barnes's "double," as it were; he is the secret sharer who suffers cruel and comical ignominy in order to demonstrate to Jake the dangers inherent in "letting go" and falling into the pit of self-deception. First we should note the similarities between Jake and "his tennis friend." They are both writers, they both fall in love with Brett Ashley, they are both superior to the meaningless swirl of drinking, promiscuity, and aimless pleasure seeking which surrounds them. Unlike the others they realize that there are stakes in the game that life has forced them to play; they are, in their different ways, equally concerned to impose meanings on their purchases and receive their money's worth. But Cohn, unlike the Count, has never "been there"; and because of the faults of his temperament, Cohn never will be there. His arrow wounds are both superficial and self-inflicted; he refuses to pay the price of self-knowledge because he has become an expert in the illusion-creating art of self-deception.

Cohn's role of "double" is cast early in the novel when he tells Jake that he can't stand to think that his life is ebbing away and he is "not really living it."

"Listen, Jake," he leaned forward on the bar. "Don't you ever get the feeling that all your life is going by and you're not taking advantage of it? Do you realize you've lived nearly half the time you have to live already?"

"Yes, every once in a while."

"Do you know that in about thirty-five years more we'll be dead?"

"What the hell, Robert," I said. "What the hell."

"I'm serious."

"It's one thing I don't worry about," I said.

"You ought to" (11).

When Cohn proposes a trip to South America, Jake tells him that "going to another country doesn't make any difference. . . . You can't get away from yourself by moving from one place to another. There's nothing to that." Cohn's adamant refusal to look nakedly at himself leaves him incapable of seeing anything external to himself with clarity. He demands that his experiences be measurable in terms of absolutes—his affair with Frances, his writing, his love for Brett; and, when his fortunes become compounded in misery, he demands absolution for his sins of misjudgment. In a remarkable scene of reverse tutorial confrontation, he begs Jake for forgiveness for his actions at Pamplona. If we remember the previously quoted conversation between Robert Jordan and Anselmo on forgiveness, it will show us how far outside the code Cohn stands:

He was crying without any noise.

"I just couldn't stand it about Brett. I've been through hell, Jake. It's been simply hell. When I met her down here Brett treated me as though I were a perfect stranger. I just couldn't stand it. We lived together at San Sebastian. I suppose you know it. I can't stand it any more."

"I guess it isn't any use," he said. "I guess it isn't any damn use."

"What?"

"Everything. Please say you forgive me Jake."

"Sure," I said. "It's all right."

"I felt so terribly. I've been through such hell, Jake. Now everything's gone. Everything" (201-2).

Robert Cohn capitulates unconditionally to the rule of *nada* through his refusal to give up his illusions; and although his intentions are far more admirable than that of the others who give in to the empty enjoyment of nothingness, his fate is to be the most despicable character that Hemingway ever created; he is similar to but worse than Richard Gordon in *To Have and Have Not.*

The delicate web of differing values is subtly suggested in the death of Vincente Girones, the twenty-eight-year-old farmer from Tafalla who has come every year to the fiesta at Pamplona to join in the *encierro,* the running of the bulls through the streets to the bull ring. Jake sees him tossed and gored as the bulls and the crowd of merrymakers sweep over and past him to the ring. When Jake returns to the café, he reports the event to the waiter:

> The waiter nodded his head and swept the crumbs from the table with his cloth.
>
> "Badly cogida," he said. "All for sport. All for pleasure. . . . A big horn wound. All for fun. Just for fun. What do you think of that?"
>
> "I don't know."
>
> "That's it. All for fun. Fun, for understand."
>
> "You're not an aficionado?"
>
> "Me? What are bulls? Animals. Brute animals. . . . You hear? Muerte. Dead. He's dead. With a horn through him. All for morning fun. Es muy flamenco."
>
> "It's bad."
>
> "Not for me," the waiter said. "No fun in that for me" (205–6).

Later Jake reports that the bull which gored Girones was killed by Pedro Romero and its ear was given to Brett, who left it with her cigarette butts in the bedside table of her hotel room. And later, after Bill has reported to Jake a full account of Cohn's activities on the night before, Jake tells him that a man had been killed in the runway outside the ring. " 'Was there?' said Bill."

This episode, deceptively trivial in its presentation, is a measure of Hemingway's control over the dramatic irony with which the novel is narrated. Girones' death is the single event of absolute human importance in the entire novel. All the infidelities, quarrels, and carousals of the principal characters fade into insubstantiality in comparison with the man who "lay face down in the trampled mud." Even the courage and dexterity with which Romero performs in the ring becomes a theatrical gesturing in contrast to the finality and absurdity of this immutable death. And Bill's incapacity to react humanly to that death is a telling indication of his (and the others') deficiencies in a full knowledge and understanding of the code.

For Girones is a symbol of the fatal and unchangeable stakes that are involved in the game that all the characters are playing. He leaves his wife and two children to run with the bulls, but he must pay with his life for his "fun." Like Robert Cohn, Girones is tossed and gored; it is probable that he dies "full of illusions"; but, in terms of the code, he fails to get his money's worth for his death. Bill and the others have become practised in ignoring the prices they will have to pay for their "fun" also. The consequences of their variety of self-deceit is a constant death-in-life because they have chosen to accept the rule of "nothingness," becoming servitors to its reign in the frenzy of their acceptance. Girones' death is the physical fact of their living deaths, and their inability to respond to it establishes clearly to what extent they have died.

Here we should perhaps deal with Brett's famous act of self-abnegation, her decision to send Romero away because she will not be "one of these bitches that ruins children." In terms of the dramatic context of the novel, her action is meant to be taken seriously; and it leads directly to the definition of morality which Hemingway later voiced in his own person in *Death in the Afternoon*:

"You know I feel rather damned good, Jake."
"You should."
"You know it makes one feel rather good deciding not to be a bitch."
"Yes."
"It's sort of what we have instead of God."
"Some people have God," I said. "Quite a lot."
"He never worked very well with me" (256-57).

It is too easily possible, I believe, to accept this scene at face value and to forget that it is filtered through Jake's narration and that its fictional meaning will depend on the values with which Jake colors it. In our earlier discussion of the code, we noticed that Hemingway demanded certain basic prerequisites from his characters before he would allow their emotional reactions to be considered worthy gauges of morality. They would have to have learned the hard way what the stakes in the game involved, and they would have to be willing to shed their illusions in their fight to force meaning out of life. It is difficult to feel that Brett meets these qualifications. She has had an unenviable time with her previous husband; she claims to be in love with Jake; she is a near-alcoholic and a near-nymphomaniac. At the end of the novel she casts her lot—whether permanent or temporary it is impossible to determine—with Mike who has made a career out of irresponsibility. What we know of Brett is what Jake chooses to divulge, and his position makes him a considerably biased observer.

He tells himself at one point that she thinks she is in love with him because he is something that she cannot have. It is certainly true that her love develops after Jake's incapacitating wound. She is ready to despise Robert Cohn because he could not believe that their stay in San Sebastian "didn't mean anything." She also has a good deal of contempt for Cohn because he allows his "suffering" to show. And yet, if we are to accept her sacrifice of Romero as an act of positive morality and in terms of her own stated code, we must judge her as severely as she judges Cohn. She cannot believe that her affair with Romero "didn't mean anything," and she makes no attempt to conceal her suffering. Jake's response to her speech on morality ("Some people have God.") may indicate his detachment from her use of the "we" in the previous sentence ("It's sort of what we have instead of God."). And similarly, the marvellously ambiguous ending of the novel would indicate Jake's holding himself apart from the illusions which Brett has voiced:

> "Oh, Jake," Brett said, "we could have had such a damned good time together."
> Ahead was a mounted policeman in khaki directing traffic. He raised his baton. The car slowed suddenly pressing Brett against me.
> "Yes," I said. "Isn't it pretty to think so?" (258-59)

But Jake has learned—in part from Count Mippipopolous—that illusions (sure beliefs projected into the future) are the first things one must discard if one wants to learn how to live life. In order to see this ambiguity more clearly, we must reinvestigate Jake's role as narrator.

When we meet Jake at the beginning of the novel he is in the process of recovering from his wound and of attempting to learn how to live with it. His days are easily occupied with the seemingly simple tasks of newspaper correspondent and café habitué;

the nights are more difficult for him to stand, since his wound, unlike the Count's, still throbs and gives him pain. He has detached himself completely from his Kansas City background and is relatively uninvolved with any of the Parisian set, although all claim him as a friend. He has three passions only: fishing, bullfighting, and Brett. The first two he is able to indulge in with full enjoyment—getting his money's worth and knowing when he has had it. The third is an impossibility on which he expends an inordinate amount of psychic energy and pain. Brett is something that he can neither afford nor even gamble for. And his meagre pleasures for the price that he pays become less and less In fact, his relationship to Brett is a pathetic parallel to Vincente Girones' with the San Fermin fiesta. Like Girones, Jake exposes himself to the dangers of being gored and of being trampled "all for fun," except that the "fun" is pain. Brett is his fiesta, as we see in the image of Brett with the white garlic wreath around her neck surrounded by the circle of *riau-riau* dancers. And the lesson that he learns from the sharp juxtaposition of his idyllic pleasures at Burguete and the misery of Pamplona is that he "was through with fiestas for a while." Just as Frederick Henry has to learn that a truly human life demands involvement or "caring-ness," so Jake Barnes must learn to become uninvolved from useless and impossible illusions if he is to remain sane.

This, it seems to me, is the point of his breaking the code of the true *aficionado* that loses him the respect of Montoya. Hemingway tells us that "Aficion means passion. An aficionado is one who is passionate about bullfights." But, as we have seen, Hemingway extends the concept of *aficion* to include the "passion" which the code requires for an honest confrontation of *nada*. And thus Jake falls from the ethics of the code badly in his arranging of the liaison between Brett and Romero. Montoya, who could forgive anything of one who had *aficion*, cannot forgive the *aficionado* who has degraded his passion. In pursuing the vain illusion of Brett, Jake too succumbs to self-deception and self-treachery, since he throws away a self-respect which he does not need to lose. His decision to remain at San Sebastian and the descriptions of his restrained enjoyment in swimming, walking, reading, and eating are reminiscent of his controlled pleasures while fishing in Burguete. His comments on himself, after sending an answer to Brett's telegram, are not just ironic; they are revelatory of the lesson he is learning: "That was it.

Send a girl off with one man. Introduce her to another to go off with him. Now go and bring her back. And sign the wire with love. That was it all right." Here, even under the disguise of self-dramatization, he is facing the truth of his actions and preparing himself for his renunciation of the impossible illusion that Brett represents. In this context his description of his arrival in Madrid has strong symbolic overtones of the decision that is on the verge of coalescence: "The Norte station in Madrid is the end of the line. All trains finish there. They don't go on anywhere." Jake too has reached the end of the line with this "vanity" that has sapped his emotional strength.

In the ensuing conversation with Brett, Jake's role is that of the "counterpuncher." His answers to her remarks are restrained and couched in a defensive irony which protects his detachment without exposing him to attack. His appetite at Botin's is keen; and although he feels the need to brace himself with wine, this is more an act of propitiation to the pain of his disseverance from an old self than a capitulation to despair. And in the final ambiguous lines which we have quoted earlier, the detachment is made complete. The policeman directing traffic raises his baton in a wonderfully suggestive gesture, both phallic and symbolic of the new command that Jake has issued to himself; and the car in which he and Brett are riding slows down suddenly. "Yes. Isn't it pretty to think so?" commemorates Jake's separate peace with himself and his new determination to live his life by those passions which are within the scope of his powers and conducive to the possibilities of his self-realization in his pursuit of them.

The structure and the ironic narrative perspective of *The Sun Also Rises* are thus the subtle explicator and shaper of its meanings. Remembering Hemingway's explanation of the three acts of the bullfight, we can find the hint of a parallel in the three-book division into which *The Sun Also Rises* falls. Book One is " the trial of the lances," in which Jake is painfully "pic-ed" by the barbs of his unresignable desire for a free expression of his natural wants; Book Two, the act of the bandilleras at Pamplona, goads him beyond endurance into jealousy and self-betrayal; and Book Three, the final division of death, is the brave administering of *quietus* to that part of his life desire which he must learn to live without if he is to live at all. The mode of narration in which the "lesson" of self-growth is presented obliquely and almost beneath the conscious awareness of the narrator-protagonist creates the problem of interpretation, but it also insures the vitality and ironic tensions within which the novel changes its shape and suggests multiple meanings. Jake is both sympathetic and reliable narrator ultimately, but his emergence as a full-fledged, graduating tyro hero is gained only after he has fallen several times, forced himself to admit his failures to himself, and secured his own forgiveness. As we have seen in our previous discussions of Hemingway's fiction, it is "the irony of the unsaid" that says most clearly and resonantly what the stripped usable values are, and what one has to pay for them.

On this base of interpretation we must now look briefly at a wider range of meanings that may explain the power and popular success of this novel. Surely the "story" we have outlined above is too bleak and spare in itself to have generated the response and wide acclamation that *The Sun Also Rises* has received since its publication. For this novel, more than any other of Hemingway's, has been cherished as a cultural document—a work of art which makes that miraculous conjunction with the spirit of the times so as to seem both distillation and artistic resolution of the prevailing temper of the age out of which it rises. Oscar Cargill points to one obvious source of its cultural appeal in his *Intellectual America*:[3] "*The Sun Also Rises* has no peer among American books that have attempted to take account of the cost of the War upon the morals of the War generation and . . . [there are] no better polemics against war than this, which was meant for no polemic at all."

Coming four years after Eliot's *The Waste Land* and three years before Faulkner's *The Sound and the Fury*, *The Sun Also Rises*—like its two peers in American writing of the 1920's— succeeds in merging the unique psychological crisis of its author with the cultural crisis of its time. "After such knowledge what forgiveness?" is perhaps the agonizing question that informs the best writings of the 1920's. World War I had been the catalytic agent in releasing the stark factor of nothingness and absurdity at the very root of traditional values. And the theme which powerfully insinuates itself into the best literary documents of the postwar period is the theme of the emotional paralysis with which sensitivity is overwhelmed at the hideous realization that life makes no sense except in those tenuous designs which enervated man himself imposes upon it. It is within the reverberations of this theme that *The Sun Also Rises* transcends its idiosyncrasies of unrepresentative locale and its restricted range of action to become a compelling and universalized metaphor for its era as well as ours.

The cause and the nature of Jake Barnes's wound force his experiences into a level of symbolic relevance which makes his slow, uncertain struggle to regain a positive stance toward life as much a parable as an "epistemological" romance. It is "the dirty war" that has crippled him, just as it has indirectly crippled the others who fritter and burn in the hells of the *bal musette* and in the pandemonic stampede of the *encierro*. Without the war as a causative background these would be merely empty and sick people who drain their lives away into the receding blue notes of a jazz orchestra; but the war was a fact, and it was one which stripped the veil of pious sanctimony and patriotic veneer from the spurious moralities and ethics of traditional American "boosterism" in religion, philosophy, and politics. The expatriates of *The Sun Also Rises* are sensitive recorders of the shock which they have suffered and of the distance that has been created between themselves and those back in America who "lived in it [*nada*] and never felt it."

As characters who are truly "ex-patriated," they live in another country where all the stuffed values of the past in which they were trained are dead: " 'You're an expatriate. You've lost touch with the soil. You get precious. Fake European standards have ruined you. You drink yourself to death. You become obsessed by sex. You spend all your time talking, not working. You're an expatriate, see? You hang around cafés' " (118).

And while it is true, as we have seen in our analysis of the hierarchy of exchange value in *The Sun Also Rises*, that the war and the consequent moral vacuum were mere excuses, for many of these "expatriates," for a life of empty sensationalism with the flimsy justification of arrogance and revolt, yet it is also true that for some—and especially Jake—the stock market of morality has crashed and the bottom has fallen out of an instinctive *rationale* for life.

For *The Sun Also Rises* is a good deal more than a polemic against war. It does show the battle casualties, and it does demonstrate that others than those in the direct line of fire were grievously crippled by flying shell fragments. But far beyond this, and much more important, it is a reassertion of the basic truth of American culture (integral to that culture, if too frequently buried under concealing platitudes) that individual man is the puny maker of his meanings in life. If he does not impose them out of an integrity to the unvarnished truths of his own experience, then they will not exist at all—and un-meaning will flood into the vacuum of his irresolution. The "wilderness" of eighteenth-century American literature and the unfathomable "frontier" of the nineteenth century fuse and echo hollowly in the *nada* of the twentieth century, but the challenge is the same and the possible creative responses to that challenge are just as limited in number. It was probably a fortuitous accident that Hemingway's personal wound and rela-tionship of estrangement from the Booth Tarkington *mores* of Oak Park should result in the compelling symbolism of *The Sun Also Rises,* but such are the graces of literary history.

Jake Barnes's wound paralyzes him at the roots of his being. He has the desire to act, coupled with a hypersensitive capacity to react; but he cannot make appropriate responses because his powers of creativity—his powers of self-generation—have atrophied as the symbolic result of his wound. He is not unlike Eliot's Gerontion or his Fisher-King who sit in despair, praying for the miracle of rain. Nor is he wholly unlike Faulkner's Quentin Compson whose similar despair and similar incapacity result from his inability to rid himself of a burdensome, life-denying past. But on a symbolic level, Jake's struggle is not ineffectual; and, it is in profound harmony with earlier American literary struggles with despair before the confrontation of nothingness. He creates his own miracle of rain, irrigating his dead lands out of the fructifying love of life to which his passion for nature (Burguete) and his admiration for human heroism (the bullfights) testify. And he is able to force himself to a new beginning, eradicating the determinism of his past—his wound, his self-treachery and degeneration with Brett—through self-forgiveness and faith in his own human resources which, like the earth, "abideth forever" in the granite veins of humanity.

Thus, *The Sun Also Rises* combines in one radical metaphor the two antithetical halves of the broad humanistic tradition that goes back to Ecclesiastes. It documents in full, unsparing detail the meaningless ant lives of petty, ephemeral humanity making its small noise of pleasure and sacrifice in the boundless and unheeding auditorium of eternity: "Vanity of vanities, saith the Preacher, vanity of vanities; all is vanity. What profit hath a man of all his labour which he taketh under the sun? One generation passeth away, and another generation cometh; but the earth abideth forever. The sun also ariseth, and the sun goeth down, and hasteth to his place where he arose."

And yet, without compromising this merciless vision of the compounded vanities by which even the best of the human race lives, Hemingway erects a tenuous but believable bridge across the shadow of nothingness in Jake Barnes's determined wrestle for meaning. The title of the novel pays its just obeisance to the cynical wisdom of the ancient Hebraic Preacher of Ecclesiastes; but in its exhortatory and unillusioned chronicling of man's heroic powers to create values out of himself, it also echoes Emerson's similar considered faith that "The sun shines to-day also."

CHAPTER 8

Hemingway: Man, Artist, and Legend

I

IT IS THE TASK of the last chapter of a book on a major writer to sum up what has been said and to attempt to indicate the nature and the extent of the writer's achievements and significance. Hemingway's work is still too fresh and close to us to be snugly categorized in literary history, but I do think that we have demonstrated a configuration of very probable shapes and designs which future Hemingway criticism and scholarship is likely to extend, refurbish, and correct. Two items, in particular, which have emerged from our study I should like to re-emphasize, because I think they are basic to an understanding and appreciation of Hemingway's peculiar merits; and, oddly enough, both of these items have frequently been neglected or distorted in the bulk of Hemingway criticism. These are the profound *organicism* of his total work and the integral relationship of his achievement to the "classic" American literary tradition. Although I have argued these positions implicitly (and sometimes, surreptitiously) within the body of the book, it will be helpful to restate them more formally.

In his "A Portrait of Mister Papa," Malcolm Cowley describes Hemingway's technique of writing:[1] ". . . he writes a book like an exploring expedition setting out into unknown territory. He knows his approximate goal, but the goal can change. He knows his direction, but he doesn't know how far he will travel or what he will find on a given day's journey." Cowley's metaphor is an interesting choice because it echoes the title, *The Undiscovered Country*, which Hemingway elected provisionally for *For Whom the Bell Tolls*;[2] and it also echoes the image, "in another country," which we have seen to be rich in connotations and possibilities in Hemingway's work. And in our discussion of the "inner symbolic drama" of Chapter III, as well as in the explications of "Big Two-Hearted River" and of *The Old Man and the Sea,* we saw that, more often than not, Hemingway's fictions seem rooted in his journeys into himself much more clearly and obsessively than is usually the case with major fictional writers. I have suggested, indeed, that the real subject of his fictions is almost always an exposition of his dynamic relation to the world at the time that he is writing. In Cowley's terms, Hemingway's writing is an exploring expedition into the unknown territory which comprises those deeper layers of awareness that the act of creativity may sometimes release. And if there is truth in these conjectures, they may illuminate the extraordinarily "round" shape which Hemingway's work makes.

In our successive analyses of style, structure, thematic interest, and treatment of time, I hope it became clear that each of these single prose techniques was subordinate and functional to an overriding purpose; that no single one of them developed its rhythms or designs out of the runaway braggadocio of a virtuoso performance. Hemingway's style has been frequently singled out for praise or derision; his metaphysic of time has been commented upon; his particular concern with violence and brutality has become identified in the popular mind with his work as a whole; and it has been imitated by literally legions of writers. The clipped, understated dialogue and the pervasive irony of perspective which he introduced in the 1920's effected a major shift in the direction that prose fiction took after the 1920's.

But no criticism, hostile or favorable, of any isolated aspect of his work throws any real light on what those works really are, because each aspect—when he is at his best—is a single functionary in the total aesthetic communication of his vision. The style is the man, but the style is also the structure and the metaphysic of time and the code and the thematic use of certain material. Perhaps half a dozen times in Hemingway's writing career, these individual elements fused into a magical symbolic construction where each is indistinguishable from the other. These are his great achievements but their individual parts can no more be approached in isolation from the others than can a Shakespearean sonnet be judged on the basis of its diction or its imagery alone. And even in the bulk of Hemingway's work where the total fusion does not quite take place, these technical functionaries are still single instruments toward the effecting of his purpose.

The organic quality of Hemingway's fiction, it seems to me, is an inevitable product of a writer who typically and intensively turned his view *internally* when he wrote. He did not write stories to promulgate a code of heroism or to exhibit an eccentrically manicured prose style or to provide sensationalistic images for the titillation of those in his audience who never left Oak Park. His writing was his way of approaching his identity—of discovering himself in the projected metaphors of his experience. He believed that, if he could see himself clear and whole, his vision might be useful to others who also lived in his world. However, in order to project those metaphors cleanly ("without faking"), he had to subject the total techniques of his writing to the natural rhythms of his own personality.

On this level, all the devices that compose his fictions must succumb to the tyrannous eye and control of "the meter-making argument"—the shaping spirit which creates form out of experience and ideally allows no intruding elements to falsify that form and betray that experience. In *Death in the Afternoon* Hemingway seems to be pointing to this ideal in his retort to Aldous Huxley:

> If a writer can make people live there may be no great characters in his book, but it is possible that his book will remain as a whole; as an entity; as a novel. . . . No matter how good a phrase or a simile he may have if he puts it in where it is not absolutely necessary and irreplaceable he is spoiling his work for egotism. Prose is architecture, not interior decoration, and the Baroque is over. . . . People in a novel . . . must be projected from the writer's assimilated experience, from his knowledge, from his head, from his heart and from all there is of him. If he ever has luck as well as seriousness and gets them out entire they will have more than one dimension and they will last a long time (191).

And whatever else it may mean, the profound resultant *organicism* of his work is an indication that Hemingway had the "seriousness" if not always the "luck."

From this viewpoint the oft-repeated criticisms of individual components of his work—style, code, etc.—fail to deal with their stated targets in an essential way, for they fail to appreciate how each is conditioned and controlled by the other accompanying techniques. It is absurdly easy to parody Hemingway's prose style; it is very difficult to parody Hemingway. It is similarly easy to extract a Hemingway "code" from his fiction to demonstrate its "primitivism," or "sadism," or "masochism," or sheer adolescence; I have tried in chapters V and VI to defend the code from such attacks and to demand, at least, that it be judged aesthetically in the totality of its context. And it is the simplest of literary-critical standpoints to dismiss Hemingway as a writer who fails to demonstrate a "development" in his work—although such criticisms rarely make it clear what a "development" is and why it is a good thing.[3] I should suppose that a "development" might mean that the "idea-content" of a writer's work exhibits a processive change over a period of years accompanied by an experimental variation in stylistic devices to record that change. If this is "development," I think that our examination of the changes and deepening of complexity which we noticed in the comparison of "The Undefeated" with *The Old Man and the Sea* would make it clear that Hemingway's work developed in clarity and complexity as his hoard of experience became richer.

But the critics of Hemingway's "arrested development" impose their own definitions of what "idea-content" in a work of art consists of; and, having fashioned an arbitrary inner sanctum of artistic excellence, they patronizingly or apologetically proclaim his failure to attain entrance to it. They usually make the false assumption that "idea-content" must mean an interest in and a capacity to dramatize conceptual "ideas." In practice they demand that Hemingway's work demonstrate a linear development (a "maturation") in the figuring forth of those philosophical or sociological concepts which the particular critic feels passionate about. But, as we have seen, this demand is to require of Hemingway's art a content which it does not possess naturally and, further, to require of art in general a special talent which would almost automatically exclude from first-class achievement such writers as Emerson and Whitman, the Shakespeare of the sonnets, and most of the British Romantic poets. Like them, Hemingway wrote his fictions out of a research into himself, trusting to the shock of emotional recognition to tell him when he had located that recondite self, and trusting further in the organic rhythms of his own nature to blend the techniques of his craft into a clean and "whole" artistic vehicle of communication. Hence the profound *organicism* of his total form and content—itself a product of the organic relation which his life imposed on his literary products—must be taken into account if his work is to be judged in terms of what it is, rather than what some special interest decides that it should have been.

And I have also stressed Hemingway's integral attachment to the basic American literary tradition as the "place" in which his achievements can most properly and fruitfully be appreciated. Hemingway characteristically confused this issue with his *ex cathedra* remarks on the "classic" American authors of the nineteenth century in *Green Hills of Africa;* in it he allowed a position of status to Mark Twain, Henry James, and Stephen Crane but disposed of Emerson, Melville, Hawthorne, and their like. We may defend him partially by suggesting that his job was to be a writer rather than a literary historian or critic, but from my standpoint the whole sequence of literary evaluations is just another indication of Hemingway's incompetence in the handling of abstractions foreign to his immediate experience.

At any rate, as I see Hemingway's relation to the American tradition, there is no question of "influence" in any direct way. I think he was the type of writer who, like Emerson, had an enormous talent for picking up what he needed (largely as a substantiation of what he already knew intuitively); he read omnivorously, seeking a reflection of himself and his immediate needs; and he was as likely to find these reflections in one place as in another. Thus, when he responds to a question of influence with the following list of culture heroes drawn from the areas of literature, music, painting, and religious mysticism, I think he is being honest as well as puckishly playful: [4] "Mark Twain, Flaubert, Stendhal, Bach, Turgenev, Tolstoi, Dostoevski, Chekhov, Andrew Marvell, John Donne, Maupassant, the good Kipling, Thoreau, Captain Marryat, Shakespeare, Mozart, Quevedo, Dante, Vergil, Tintoretto, Hieronymus Bosch, Breughel, Patinier, Goya, Giotto, Cezanne, Van Gogh, Gaugin, San Juan de la Cruz, Góngora—it would take a day to remember everyone." And when a writer is as over-influenced as the above listing suggests, it is probably more fruitful to think of him as an "original," or as almost without meaningful influences.

And yet this has been the typical situation of the American writer. Concerned ultimately with the artistic process of a quest for identity, he has used anything he could get his hands on—from books on the history of whaling to treatises of phrenological research. With some few and obvious exceptions, the major American writers have responded to literary influence as a one-way transaction. They adapt their external materials to their own obsessive uses; they adamantly resist being formed or molded by those materials. And with a writer as organic in his development as we have seen Hemingway to be, this resistance to the formative impress of influences would be particularly strong and unyielding. But Hemingway's place in that chain of great American writers that stretches from Jonathan Edwards to himself seems to me to be secure and beyond question. It is not a matter of "influence" so much as what we might almost think of as inalienable birthright. The *nada* that was the challenge and the stimulation of Hemingway's art was, as we saw in our discussion of *The Sun Also Rises*, just the new manifestation of the same *nada* that was "wilderness" for the Puritans and unknown "frontier" for the nineteenth century. The function of the American artist—we are tempted to say the "only" function of the American artist—has been to create order out of the primordial chaos that "wilderness," "frontier," or *nada* represent. And he has had to do this out of an awesome lone-liness, unsupported by the sustaining guides of religious, philosophical, or social traditions.

The chaos has been external and internal, and inexorable in its encroachments on those tenuous structures of order which individual men have erected out of their painful isolation. It has demanded an endless series of new beginnings—a constant series of creative acts which might bring *being* (identity, value) out of nothingness. The shape of the literature which has been the result of this overweening challenge has been inevitably eccentric. Its accent has been colloquial or folkloristic; its forms have tended strongly to the abstract, the symbolic, the mythic. Its social purposes have been unashamedly moralistic, aiming at a direct stimulation of the heroic image of man in the minds and hearts of its audience. To use a phrase of Emerson's that would be palatable to Puritans, Transcendentalists, and twentieth-century non-categorizables alike, it has sought to effect an "active soul" in its readers and it has used almost any means to gain this end. It has "hoaxed" and exhorted, chanted hypnotic incantations, and delivered allegorical moral sermons. It has been overtly purposive in its concern with bringing the new Adam to life; and it has also frequently disguised its concern in the form of stories of adventure, ghost tales, fables and fantasies. And it has usually been characterized by a peculiar ironic humor—sometimes as blatant as Mark Twain's, sometimes as hidden as Whitman's. In the novel this tradition has created that most flexible of literary forms, the *romance*, the ideal fictional instrument for the projection of warring states of mind, for dramatizations of the desperate grapplings for identity.[5]

That Hemingway's work can only be appreciated at the heart in terms of this tradition, I have attempted to show. His characteristic employment of fantasy projections, his faith in the validity of an *inner* rather than an outer reality, his attitudes towards *organicism* in form and content, and his employment of his writing as an instrument rather than an end would all seem to indicate that it is in this tradition of romance rather than in terms of European realism that his successes and failures be measured. And within this tradition I have suggested that the imperatives of his temperament led him toward the aesthetic resolutions of Emerson and Whitman rather than to those of Hawthorne and Melville. What we have called his "anti-intellectualistic" bias—the fact of his temperament which led him to place his reliance on the primacy of his emotions—would necessarily give him an unshakeable faith in himself, and in faith as well. And while he was, as we have seen, keenly aware of the web of multiple ironies through which reality manifests itself, his primal faith required a positive confrontation of those ironies—an act of will—rather than an indirect confrontation—an act of intellect. Hence, although the question of influences is generally irrelevant, his work should, I believe, be considered in the light of that American literary tradition of which he is an organic part as well as a brilliant continuation.

II

If one of the measures of an artist's success is the influence which he himself exerts on his contemporaries and successors, then Hemingway is certainly the most important twentieth-century writer in this respect. Although we can do little more than indicate the fact here, it would not be too much of an exaggeration to say that after 1930 no writer in any country of the world failed to feel Hemingway's influence.[6] His prose style lost very little of its power when translated into the major western languages, and the sensuous appeal of his descriptions of action made his work as popular abroad as it was in America. As early as October, 1927, he was writing to his editor, Maxwell

Perkins that he then had "2 British, 1 Danish, 1 Swedish, 1 French, and 1 German publisher."[7] His international popularity increased rather than waned throughout his lifetime, embracing the continents of Asia and Africa as well as Europe. And his translated works were more than popular; the Nobel Prize Committee justly pointed to his powers of stylistic influence when they praised his "forceful and style-making mastery of the art of modern narration."

Even in translation the superficial characteristics of his style and flexible irony proved to be incredibly contagious on writers seeking a new mode of approach to literature as well as on writers seeking a more electric appeal to a mass audience. His influence has included such serious figures as Graham Greene, André Malraux, Albert Camus, Elio Vittorini, Giuseppe Berto, James T. Farrell, and John Steinbeck. On a more widespread level, it included almost every beginning writer of the 1930's and 1940's to such an extent that creative writing workshops and classes were frequently exercises in Hemingway prose. And in the manufacture of "action-stories" for the mass media throughout the world, Hemingway's influence is and has been of enormous weight on popular journalism, "pulp" writing of all varieties, and scripts for motion pictures and television. In fact, the proliferating imitations of the superficial characteristics of his work by writers who copy his letters without capturing the forming spirit behind those letters has made it increasingly difficult for Hemingway's achievements in his own work to be judged without the dilution of this popular image. At least this explanation may account for some of the critical resistance to his art.

Hemingway's creative output over a lifetime of serious, steady writing is not very large.[8] Some fifty-five stories, two works of nonfiction, one *novella,* and six novels make up the sum. Of these his reputation will probably rest ultimately on *The Sun Also Rises, A Farewell to Arms, For Whom the Bell Tolls, The Old Man and the Sea,* and some eight to ten short stories. But actually, the volume of his work is somewhat larger than this list indicates because, as we have seen, his individual efforts have a fragmentary quality, even when they are whole within themselves. The separate stories, like the separate aspects of his fictional techniques, are, in a sense, functionaries to the composite unity of his *oeuvre.* Even when the names of the characters change and their backgrounds become slightly differentiated, there is still a sense in which each is a new unit in the fully constructed mosaic of Hemingway's life work. This is not to suggest that he created a Yoknapatawpha County in his fiction but that, as a deeply committed organic writer, the total of his efforts makes something like a fictional *Leaves of Grass*. And, as with Whitman, the impress of his individual works is cumulative in its strength and artistic subtlety.

And in the attempt to assess Hemingway's ultimate significance as a major twentieth-century writer, another factor intrudes to make his work more important than the intrinsic value which his finely wrought short stories and novels possess. Hemingway's legendary personality, as he lived it in the newspapers and in the public eye, is inextricably intertwined with his fictional themes and images. His life is in his books, as with all serious artists; but his books inevitably reflect back to his life. Unlike the works of his two great American contemporaries, Eliot and Faulkner, Hemingway's work does not stand by itself—complete, austere, impersonal, self-defined. We are not interested in a Faulknerian "hero" or an Eliotic "code"; but countless readers have accepted the Hemingway hero as a living reality, and they have subjected the Hemingway code to their own versions of employment. In Hemingway's case, his life and his literary efforts were so much of a single piece and his public life was so romantically close to the heroic derring-do of his fictional heroes that this mergence of life and literature cannot be dismissed by literary criticism. To do so would be to fail to appreciate the extraliterary dimension which Hemingway's fictions have contained for his audience. Paradoxically it may even be an aesthetic deficiency for an artist not to submerge himself completely in his work; but art is large as well as long, and Hemingway's personality will doubtless continue to be a factor in the appeal of his works, even as Mark Twain's personality persists in being so in his.

In summing up such a protean figure and such a paradoxical accomplishment, it is difficult to strike the right-sounding chord that will be just to his strengths without overrating them—and honest to his weaknesses without making them of more import than they actually are. Almost all of Hemingway's significant contemporaries possessed talents which were beyond his ability. Faulkner's fecundity of imagination and invention far surpassed his. He never learned how to dramatize and give poetic life to the abstractions of ideas as Eliot could so handsomely do. He lacked Thomas Wolfe's torrential self-confidence. He was completely without the fine sense of scenario and the light touch of wit which could bring straight exposition to life, as in F. Scott Fitzgerald's work. He did not have the dogged seriousness of vision and historical curiosity that his friend John Dos Passos possessed. He couldn't tell a story with the effortless charm that Steinbeck assumed so naturally. And he never knew how to create the kind of scene in which social normality parades in convincing figures—the kind of scene which Sinclair Lewis or John P. Marquand could do with their left hands. In fact, he lacked almost all the tools which fiction writers have traditionally employed as their basic stock in trade. He had only what seems to have been a tormented zeal to find out who he was by writing it out of himself, a measurement of personal integrity which rarely faltered, and a genius for adapting the limited resources and materials that he did possess into a brilliantly harmonic fusion.

Gertrude Stein and William Faulkner have both implied in their different ways that the great failure of Hemingway was his desire to play it safe—to stay within the limits of what he could do rather than to attempt something beyond his grasp. The perception, I think, is an acute one, for it points to the admittedly narrow range which Hemingway's accomplishments include. But the criticism in the perception misses the real point entirely, and the miss must have given Hemingway a good deal of pleasure. For although his range was limited, I doubt very much that he was playing it safe. Like Santiago, that other fisherman who knew many tricks, Hemingway went too far out in every one of his serious fictions; he extended himself beyond his resources and powers; and he fought his way home on sheer nerve and desperate faith. Part of his public role was to act as though he were a confident natural force with immeasurable reserves in store that he hadn't even made inventory of.

The silence of his last nine years, his suicide, the recurrent images in his fictions of the man that keeps the light burning at night in a vain attempt to ward off the horrors of "nothing"—all these strongly suggest that Hemingway's natural talents were "zero at the bone," and that he created himself out of that "nothing" under immense pressure in the writing of his prose. Indeed, his writing career argues cogently that whatever philosophical validity the Hemingway code may have possessed, its pragmatic functioning for him was cardinal and irrefutable.

It enabled him to take over the role of what we might call "*jongleur* of pain" that he imaged so poignantly in his description of Belmonte in the Pamplona bull ring. He exhausted himself beyond his natural means, but he maintained that "grace under pressure," which, for him, was one of the conditions from which immortality might come.

But rather than end on such a subdued note, let us remember that if his range was narrow, it was not shallow. Art is long and it is large and it can also be deep; and if the sum of Hemingway's achievement was to project in compelling symbols his own human situation, his popularity attests to the fact that his was not a unique human condition. Too fragmented to make a rebellious vain rush against life and too proud to accept the inevitability of defeat and resignation, Hemingway found in himself and communicated to countless readers a stance of heroism—positive, unillusioned, and defiantly humanistic.

Notes and References

Chapter One

1. Johnson J. Hooper, *Simon Suggs Adventures* (1845, reprinted Philadelphia, 1881), p. 26. Quoted in Pascal Covici, Jr., *Mark Twain's Humor* (Dallas, 1962), p. 7. I am indebted to Mr. Covici's analyses for much indirect stimulation.

2. Carlos Baker has been named the official biographer. The best account of the early years is Charles A. Fenton, *The Apprenticeship of Ernest Hemingway* (New York, 1954). Other useful sources include Malcolm Cowley, "A Portrait of Mister Papa," *Life*, XXV (Jan. 10, 1949), 86-101; George Plimpton, "Ernest Hemingway," *Paris Review*, XVIII (Spring, 1958), 61-82; and Lillian Ross, *Portrait of Hemingway* (New York, 1961). Among recent biographical contributions, the following reminiscences are of varying (although limited) utility: Morley Callaghan, *That Summer in Paris* (New York, 1962); Leicester Hemingway, *My Brother, Ernest Hemingway* (New York, 1962); and Marcelline Hemingway Sanford, *At the Hemingways* (Boston, 1962).

3. See Philip Young, *Ernest Hemingway* (New York, 1952), for the most thorough and persuasive examination of this aspect of his work.

4. "Homage to Hemingway," *New Republic*, LXXXVIII (Nov. 11, 1936), 40.

5. "Hemingway: Gauge of Morale," *Eight Essays* (New York, 1954), p. 102. First printed, 1941.

6. May 13, 1950. Republished as *Portrait of Hemingway* with the note that the author had no intention of presenting a derogatory portrait and that she and Hemingway were perfectly satisfied with the one presented.

7. "Not Spain But Hemingway," *Horizon, III* (May, 1941), 360.

8. See "American Bohemians in Paris A Weird Lot," *Toronto Star Weekly*, March 25, 1922; quoted in Fenton, pp. 124-25. See also *Green Hills of Africa* (New York, 1935), pp. 19-27, for a good specimen of a Hemingway pronouncement.

9. His most notorious main event was with Max Eastman (Aug. 11, 1937); see Carlos Baker, *Hemingway: The Writer as Artist* (Princeton, 1956), p. 233. For literary purposes, a more significant preliminary event may have taken place at Pamplona, July, 1925. See Harold Loeb, *The Way It Was* (New York, 1959), pp. 294-97.

10. Alfred G. Aronowitz and Peter Hamill, *Ernest Hemingway: The Life and Death of a Man* (New York, 1961), pp. 216-18.

11. See Fenton's *Apprenticeship,* Chapter I, for the best picture of Oak Park.

12. Malcolm Cowley, "Portrait," p. 99.

13. Hemingway married Hadley Richardson in 1921, divorced her in 1927 to marry Pauline Pfeiffer, was divorced by her in 1940 when he married Martha Gelhorn, and was divorced once more in 1944 to marry Mary Welsh.

14. *A Farewell to Arms* (New York, 1929), p. 196.

15. I refer here to the important distinction between *anti-intellectual* and *anti-intellectualist* which Morton White makes in "Reflections on Anti-Intellectualism," *Daedalus* (Summer, 1962), pp. 457-68.

16. See especially Wyndham Lewis, "The Dumb Ox: A Study of Ernest Hemingway," *The American Review,* III (June, 1934), 289-312. All subsequent specimens of this viewpoint are merely footnotes to this classical essay in expert vituperation.

17. Hemingway's courage has never seriously been impugned, at least not since the Max Eastman episode. His generosity with younger writers up until World War II is generally acknowledged.

18. "I have not been at all hard-boiled since July 8, 1918—on the night of which I discovered that that also was vanity." Letter to Maxwell Perkins, quoted in Baker, *Hemingway,* p. 4n.

19. See "The Adventures of Nick Adams," pp. 1-27, in Young's *Hemingway* for the most cogent exposition of the "trauma" theory.

20. *The Novel of Violence in America* (Dallas, 1957, rev. ed.), p. 194.

21. *A Farewell to Arms,* p. 350.

22. So Hemingway admitted in a letter to Baker; Baker, *Hemingway,* p. 142n.

23. Colonel Cantwell's demand for a corner table in restaurants and his consciousness of protecting his flanks in bars is an absurd extension of this. If Hemingway means this to be comical, he fails; if he means it to be serious, it cannot but be taken comically.

24. John T. Flanagan's "Hemingway's Debt to Sherwood Anderson," *The Journal of English and Germanic Philology,* LIV (October, 1955), 507-20, is a good starting place for the general relationship between Hemingway and Anderson. The Gertrude Stein feud is articulately argued in Gertrude Stein's *The Autobiography of Alice B. Toklas* (New York, 1933) and Hemingway's *Green Hills,* 65-66. The Stein rift seems to have received at least a token reconciliation during the liberation of Paris in 1944.

25. The list could be considerably longer. As representatives let these suffice: Harold Loeb, Max Eastman, Sinclair Lewis. To these could be added the generals and statesmen whom Hemingway disapproved of in *Across the River and Into the Trees.*

26. This may help to explain the insertion of such figures as counts Mippipopoulos and Greffi into *The Sun Also Rises* and in

A Farewell to Arms, since their age makes equality of relationship out of the question for either character.

27. Jake Barnes's relationship to Lady Brett is a possible exception, but biologically he is not a lover. See Baker, *Hemingway,* pp. 109-16, for a spirited but unconvincing defense of Hemingway's female characterizations. I will qualify this concerning Frederick Henry in Chapter IV, but without changing the generalization significantly.

28. The full impact of World War I on the American literary scene can hardly be indicated here. A good introduction to the period is Frederick J. Hoffman, *The Twenties* (New York, 1955).

29. Quoted in Baker, *Hemingway,* p. 71.

30. *A Farewell to Arms* averaged close to twenty thousand sold copies per month in the first four months of its appearance (Baker, *Hemingway,* p. 333).

31. By Edmund Wilson. Reprinted and commented upon in Wilson's *A Literary Chronicle, 1920-1950* (New York, 1952).

32. Sept. 5, 12, and 19 (1961).

33. The drawing-power of Hemingway's name may be indicated by a partial listing of the magazines in which he published: *Atlantic Monthly, Collier's, Cosmopolitan, Esquire, Fortune, Holiday, Ken, Life, Scribner's Magazine, Vogue.* And this was *before* it became fashionable for national magazines to peddle culture. The influence of the movie versions of Hemingway's fictions should also be taken into account.

34. *The Vanishing Hero* (London, 1956), p. 164.

35. This is an enormously large and complicated subject. See Herbert Marcuse's arguments in *Eros and Civilization* (Boston, 1955).

36. For a *tour de force* exposition on the sense of smell, see Pilar's explanation of the smell of death-to-come (*For Whom the Bell Tolls,* pp. 254-57). Hemingway can be profitably compared to Whitman ("Song of Myself") in their respective concerns with an imaginative re-creation of the five senses.

37. Benjamin Franklin and Ezra Pound are probably also exceptions: the first can be ignored here since he was not a "creative" writer in the usual sense; the second is a special case, and, at any rate, he never enjoyed a wide popularity.

38. See Wyndham Lewis, *op. cit.,* for the *anti's;* for the *pro's,* Elliot Paul, "Hemingway and the Critics," *Saturday Review of Literature,* XVII (Nov. 6, 1937), 3-4.

39. *Green Hills,* p. 109.

40. A good comprehensive view of the American literary scene in the 1930's with a special focus on Leftist movements is Daniel Aaron's *Writers on the Left* (New York, 1961).

41. Lillian Ross, *Portrait,* p. 37.

42. Quoted in Baker, *Hemingway,* p. 293n.

43. See "A Man of the World" and "Get a Seeing-Eyed Dog," Hemingway's contributions to the *Atlantic Monthly* Jubilee edition (November, 1957).

44. Ross, *Portrait*, p. 48.

45. According to Reverend D. Richard Wolfe (Columbia City, Ind.) who spent four days in close contact with Hemingway in the psychiatric ward of the Mayo Clinic (Spring, 1961), Hemingway appeared to be a man "in despair." He seemed thoroughly disoriented and spiritually listless; nor did he appear to be searching for a way out of his despair. Whether this situation was a temporary result of his treatment or something more basic, it has been impossible for me to discover. (Telephone conversation between Mr. Wolfe and the author, Aug. 28, 1962).

Chapter Two

1. Compare with Whitman: "For well dear brother I know / If thou wast not granted to sing thou would'st surely die." Whitman, of course, had never heard of the "trauma theory" of literary creativity.

2. *Death in the Afternoon*, p. 278. Two rewarding articles on Hemingway's aesthetic are Robert C. Hart, "Hemingway on Writing," *College English*, XVIII (March, 1957), 314-20; and C. Hugh Holman, "Hemingway and Emerson: Notes on the Continuity of an Aesthetic Tradition," *Modern Fiction Studies*, I: 3 (August, 1955), 12-16. I have tried to pursue Mr. Holman's direction in this book, but I am conscious of having failed. I still agree that the study is a needed one.

3. *Death in the Afternoon*, pp. 234-35.

4. Compare with Emily Dickinson's famous kinetic test for authentic poetic experience.

5. It might be argued that Hemingway uses this speech as a technique of characterization; however, as impersonal narrator and in his public statements, his sports usage is obsessively marked. See Ross, *Portrait*.

6. Pilar's recollection of Finito (*For Whom the Bell Tolls*, pp. 182-90) is similar in feeling and similar also in its dramatically intrusive character.

7. Hemingway's poem "Mitrailliatrice" (*Poetry*, January, 1923, p. 193) comes very close to suggesting that death is in the typewriter.

8. Two excellent studies of "Snows" are: Oliver Evans, " 'The Snows of Kilimanjaro': A Revaluation," *PMLA*, LXXVI (December, 1961), 601-7; Marion Montgomery, "The Leopard and the Hyena: Symbol and Meaning in 'The Snows of Kilimanjaro,' " *The University of Kansas City Review*, XXVII (Summer, 1961), 277-82.

9. Robert O. Stephens points out ("Hemingway's Riddle of Kilimanjaro: Idea and Image," *American Literature*, XXXII, January, 1961) that Hemingway adapted the epigraph from Hans Meyer,

Across East African Glaciers, changing the antelope in the original to a leopard.

10. Hemingway takes special care to emphasize that Harry is not just thinking of writing, but actually is writing. " 'I've been writing,' he said. 'But I got tired.' " Immediately after that the death-hyena climbs on his chest.

11. Hemingway made a practice of referring to the lucrative movie version as "The Snows of Zanuck." See his African articles in *Look.*

12. Ross, *Portrait,* p. 56.

13. *Green Hills of Africa,* p. 20.

14. Fenton's *Apprenticeship* is the most valuable source for any work on Hemingway's formative years. For the Lardner relationship see pp. 22-26.

15. Fenton, Chapters II, IV, and following.

16. Quoted in Baker, *Hemingway,* p. 25.

17. Wilson, *The Shores of Light,* (New York, 1952), p. 117.

18. A fine discussion of the Stein relationship is in Fenton, *Apprenticeship,* pp. 150-58.

19. Two illuminating articles on Hemingway's style are: John Graham, "Ernest Hemingway: The Meaning of Style," *Modern Fiction Studies,* VI (Winter, 1960-61), 298-313; Harry Levin, "Observations on the Style of Ernest Hemingway," *Kenyon Review,* XIII (Autumn, 1951), 581-609.

20. "Hemingway," *Kenyon Review,* IX (Winter, 1947), 28.

21. *Hemingway,* p. 155.

22. The distinction can be suggested by a comparison between the African landscapes of *Green Hills of Africa* and the same landscapes in "The Snows of Kilimanjaro" and in "The Short Happy Life of Francis Macomber." In spite of Hemingway's most strenuous efforts, the background in the first book is unconvincing and un-alive, but it becomes almost an active character in the short stories. The difficulty with *Green Hills* is the absence of any significant tension, or forcefield, to bring places into a focus. It is very hard for a reader to become terribly concerned about whether Hemingway's friend Karl does or does not shoot a bigger kudu than Hemingway.

23. "Hemingway and The Image of Man," *Partisan Review,* XX: 3 (1953), 342. Bellow's comment strikes me as a most accurate prophecy and interpretation of Hemingway's suicide.

Chapter Three

1. Hemingway is reputed to have written poetry throughout his career, and presumably poems are among his papers. Marlene Dietrich once said somewhere that his poems were "beautiful," but she did not divulge her standards of evaluation.

2. For a more thorough explication of this subject, see my "The

Shape of American Poetry," *Jahrbüch für Amerikastudien,* Band 6. 1961, pp. 122-33

3. Philip Young's chapter, "The Hero and the Code," *op. cit.,* is an excellent introduction. See also Delmore Schwartz, "Ernest Hemingway's Literary Situation," *The Southern Review,* III: 4 (Spring, 1938), 769-82; and Warren, *op. cit.,* for good analyses of the code.

4. Ernest Hemingway, "The Denunciation," *Esquire,* X (November, 1938), 112.

5. Baker, *Hemingway,* p. 131.

6. One could argue that the bull in "The Undefeated" and the lion in "The Short Happy Life of Francis Macomber" are perfectly representative "tutors" in action. Hemingway's rendition of their thoughts is at least as intelligent as those of Manuel.

7. Young, *Hemingway,* p. 36.

8. Two excellent discussions of this phase of modern fiction are Ihab Hassan, *Radical Innocence* (Princeton, 1961) and R. W. B. Lewis, *The Picaresque Saint* (New York, 1959).

9. A possible exception to the rule is Schatz in "A Day's Wait."

10. Baker's discussion in his *Hemingway,* pp. 283-87, is especially valuable on this subject.

11. There is actually a further confusion in the end of the novel in which Henry identifies with his stillborn son ("Poor little kid. I wished the hell I'd been choked like that"); he also rejects himself as father, claiming that he has no feeling of fatherhood. The most interesting detail is his looking into a mirror with his white gown and beard: "I looked in the glass and saw myself looking like a fake doctor with a beard." Dr. Clarence Hemingway, and presumably Dr. Adams as well, wore beards.

12. Baker, *Hemingway,* p. 97.

13. The dates of the publication of *To Have and Have Not* are a little confusing. Two sections of the novel first appeared as short stories: "One Trip Across," in April, 1934; and "The Tradesman's Return," in February, 1936. The novel was published in October, 1937, with the third Harry Morgan section written seemingly in the spring or summer of 1937.

14. For purposes of simplification I have ignored the money motif in this story, as well as in "The Snows of Kilimanjaro." The Freudian-minded critic can doubtless find a rich harvest in Hemingway's references to wealth and money.

15. Baker, *Hemingway,* footnotes on pp. 238-39.

Chapter Four

1. There are also numerous fictions of Hemingway which do not fall into any of these forms; in general, they are among his lesser achievements. These would include such works as *The Torrents of*

Spring, "Mr. and Mrs. Elliot," "A Canary for One," and "Homage to Switzerland." In his exceptional stories Hemingway seems to be playing with a more directly satirical approach to fiction.

2. Philip Young's discussion of this story (*Hemingway,* pp. 15-20ff.) is particularly illuminating and provocative.

3. The Harry Morgan sections of *To Have and Have Not* are also variants of the tutor story.

4. Broch's discussion of this point, as well as his description of the "style of old age," are extraordinarily relevant to *The Old Man and the Sea.* See his introduction to Rachel Bespaloff's *On the Iliad* (New York, 1947).

5. Two careful and useful readings of *The Old Man and the Sea* are: Clinton S. Burhans, Jr., "*The Old Man and the Sea*: Hemingway's Tragic Vision of Man," *American Literature,* XXXI (January, 1960), 446-55; Robert O. Stephens, "Hemingway's Old Man and the Iceberg," *Modern Fiction Studies,* VII: 4 (Winter, 1961-62), 295-304.

6. "An Interview with Ernest Hemingway," reprinted in Carlos Baker, *Hemingway and His Critics* (New York, 1961), p. 29.

7. The remark is quoted in Baker, *Hemingway,* p. 323n.

8. See Chapter II, note 2.

9. It is an interesting commentary on Transcendentalism that Hawthorne, in so many ways hostile to its precepts, should give the most lucid fictional expositions of its principles. See also "The Great Stone Face."

10. A more thorough and comprehensive explanation of "the epistemological story" is attempted in my "American Literature and 'The American Experience,'" *American Quarterly,* XIII: 2 (Summer, 1961), 115-25.

11. There is a large amount of useful commentary on *A Farewell to Arms.* Particularly valuable are: Baker, *Hemingway,* pp. 94-116; Norman Friedman, "Criticism and the Novels," *Antioch Review,* XVIII (Fall, 1958), 343-70; and James F. Light, "The Religion of Death in *A Farewell to Arms,*" *Modern Fiction Studies* VII: 2 (Summer, 1961), 169-73.

12. Ferguson occupies an almost Jamesian role in this novel, serving as norm of commonsense or as guide to the obvious. Remembering Mark Twain's abuse of the guide Ferguson in *Innocents Abroad,* it is possible that Hemingway is having a private joke in his naming and employment of this character.

13. The remark is quoted in Baker, *Hemingway,* p. 98n.

Chapter Five

1. My conscious indebtedness in the following discussion is to the thinking of Hannah Arendt, and particularly to her book, *The Human Condition* (Chicago, 1958); peripheral to it, but not without influence,

is Hazel E. Barnes's *The Literature of Possibility* (Lincoln, Neb., 1959).

2. There seems to be a basic inconsistency in the dialogue of this story so that it is impossible to be sure who is talking to whom in several crucial places. See William E. Colburn, "Confusion in 'A Clean Well-Lighted Place,'" *College English,* XX (February, 1959), 241-42; and F. P. Kroeger, "The Dialogue in 'A Clean Well-Lighted Place,'" *College English,* XX (February, 1959), 240-41.

3. Baker, *Hemingway,* p. 124. Professor Baker's discussion of this story is very interesting and provocative.

4. An excellent discussion on this point is Joseph Beaver's "'Technique' in Hemingway," *College English,* XIV (March, 1953), 325-28.

5. *The Withered Branch* (London, 1950). The excerpts are on pages 24, 27, and 31.

6. "American Novelists in French Eyes," *Atlantic Monthly* (August, 1946), p. 118. Relevant discussion of Hemingway's influence on Camus would include Richard Lehan, "Camus and Hemingway," *Wisconsin Studies in Contemporary Literature,* I: 2 (1960), 37-48; and Philip Thody, "A Note on Camus and the American Novel," *Comparative Literature,* IX (Summer, 1957), 243-49.

Chapter Six

1. Among the studies on Hemingway's handling of time, I found the following of special interest and utility: Frederick I. Carpenter, "Hemingway Achieves the Fifth Dimension," *PMLA,* LXIX (September, 1954), 711-18; John Graham, *op. cit.;* and Sean O'Faolain, *op. cit.* Attempts to relate Hemingway's metaphysic of time to that of Henri Bergson I have ignored, not because I dispute the affinities in the two schemes, but because I think that equal affinities exist between Hemingway's use of time and Emerson's.

2. Levin, *op. cit.,* p. 109.

3. Among the many interesting readings of *For Whom the Bell Tolls,* the following are representative: Baker, *op. cit.,* pp. 223-63; Maxwell Geismar, *Writers in Crisis* (Boston, 1942), pp. 79-84; and William T. Moynihan, "The Martyrdom of Robert Jordan," *College English,* XXI (December, 1959), 127-32.

4. A very interesting study of Hemingway's dialogue in this novel is Edward Fenimore, "English and Spanish in *For Whom the Bell Tolls,* ELH, X (1943), 73-86. See also Arturo Barea, *op. cit.*

Chapter Seven

1. Baker, *op. cit.,* p. 81.

2. Two especially penetrating readings of *The Sun Also Rises* are Frederick J. Hoffman, *op. cit.;* and Mark Spilka, "The Death of

Love in *The Sun Also Rises*," *Twelve Original Essays in Great American Novels* (Detroit, 1958), pp. 238-56. Other interesting interpretations are Baker, *op. cit.*, pp. 75-93; Arthur L. Scott, "In Defense of Robert Cohn," *College English*, XVIII (March, 1957), 309-14; and Robert O. Stephens, "Hemingway's Don Quixote in Pamplona," *College English*, XXIII (December, 1961), 216-18. And, if only as an interpretative curiosity, see R. W. Stallman, *The Houses that James Built* (East Lansing, 1961), pp. 173-99.

3. Cargill, (New York, 1948), pp. 357-58.

Chapter Eight

1. Cowley, *op. cit.*, p. 94.

2. Baker, *Hemingway*, p. 239n.

3. There are many specimens of this over-all attack on Hemingway. A particularly good example because it contains almost all of the anti-Hemingway shibboleths in a wonderfully patronizing dress is Dwight Macdonald's "Ernest Hemingway," *Encounter*, XVIII (January, 1962), 115-21. This article is also of interest because it shows how easy it is to parody Hemingway's style while capturing none of his seriousness or his concern with truth.

4. Plimpton, *op. cit.*, p. 27.

5. For a fuller exposition of this American literary tradition, see my "American Literature and 'The American Experience,' " *op. cit.;* and see also Richard Chase, *The American Novel and Its Tradition* (New York, 1957); Daniel G. Hoffman, *Form and Fable in American Fiction* (New York, 1961); Charles Feidelson, Jr., *Symbolism and American Literature* (Chicago, 1953); and R. W. B. Lewis, *The American Adam* (Chicago, 1955).

6. For an indication of Hemingway's influence on an international level see the following: Baker, *Hemingway and His Critics, op. cit.*, pp. 1-18; Deming Brown, "Hemingway in Russia," *American Quarterly*, V (1953), 143-56; Mario Praz, "Hemingway in Italy," *Partisan Review*, XV (1948), 1086-1100; and the *In Memoriam* tribute in *Saturday Review* (July 29, 1961) which contains remarks by Salvador de Madariaga, Frank Moraes, Carlo Levi, Ilya Ehrenburg, and Alan Pryce-Jones. The tribute in *Der Spiegel*, Vol. 29 (July 12, 1961), pp. 45-52, not only suggests Hemingway's significance in Germany, but is one of the best journalistic surveys of his life and work.

7. Baker, *Hemingway and His Critics, op. cit.*, p. 1.

8. There have been persistent rumors since the late 1940's that Hemingway was working on a "big" book dealing with the "land, sea, and air." After the publication of *The Old Man and the Sea*, it was reported that the *novella* was the coda to that big book, comprising roughly one-sixth of the whole (see Baker, *Hemingway, op. cit.*,

p. 295n.); no one seems to know what has happened to the other five-sixths. I have been unable to verify or refute these rumors. Scribner's announced after Hemingway's death that it had had in its possession in 1960 two almost completed book-length manuscripts. One was a series of reminiscences of the 1920's with chapters dealing with Scott Fitzgerald, Ezra Pound, Gertrude Stein, "and many other people, places and things"; the other was an expansion of "The Dangerous Summer" articles that appeared in *Life* on September 5, 12, and 19, 1960 (*Publishing Report*, I, 2, [Nov. 6, 1961]). Hemingway's total effects were shipped to a bonded warehouse in the United States, but to my knowledge these effects have yet to be examined. They certainly must contain a mine of extremely valuable material, but I have my doubts that they will substantially affect the nature of Hemingway's achievement. Still, he was a shifty man with many "tricks," and we cannot be sure of what surprises are in store for us.

Selected Bibliography

PRIMARY SOURCES

The following list includes only the major publications. The reader is referred to Carlos Baker's *Hemingway: The Writer as Artist* (Princeton, 1956) for a listing of uncollected items of both fiction and nonfiction. Items appearing after 1956 can be found in *The Reader's Guide to Periodical Literature*.

Three Stories and Ten Poems. Paris: Contact Publishing Company, 1923.
in our time. Paris: Three Mountains Press, 1924.
In Our Time. New York: Boni and Liveright, 1925.
The Torrents of Spring. New York: Charles Scribner's Sons, 1926.
The Sun Also Rises. New York: Charles Scribner's Sons, 1926.
Men Without Women. New York: Charles Scribner's Sons, 1927.
A Farewell to Arms. New York: Charles Scribner's Sons, 1929.
Death in the Afternoon. New York: Charles Scribner's Sons, 1932.
Winner Take Nothing. New York: Charles Scribner's Sons, 1933.
Green Hills of Africa. New York: Charles Scribner's Sons, 1935.
To Have and Have Not. New York: Charles Scribner's Sons, 1937.
The Spanish Earth. Cleveland: J. B. Savage Company, 1938.
The Fifth Column and the First Forty-nine Stories. New York: Charles Scribner's Sons, 1938.
For Whom the Bell Tolls. New York: Charles Scribner's Sons, 1940.
Across the River and Into the Trees. New York: Charles Scribner's Sons, 1950.
The Old Man and the Sea. New York: Charles Scribner's Sons, 1952.

SECONDARY SOURCES

Bibliographical Materials

BEEBE, MAURICE, "Criticism of Ernest Hemingway: A Checklist with an Index to Studies of Separate Works," *Modern Fiction Studies*, I (August, 1955), 36-45. This is the first checklist of criticism, quite thorough, and usefully arranged.
COHN, LOUIS H. *A Bibliography of the Works of Ernest Hemingway*. New York: Random House, 1931. An indispensable tool for serious study of the writings in the 1920's.
SAMUELS, LEE. *A Hemingway Check List*. New York: Charles Scribner's Sons, 1951. This updates the Cohn listings to date of publication.

Selected Bibliography

WALKER, WARREN S. "Ernest Hemingway," *Twentieth-Century Short Story Explication*. Hamden, Connecticut: The Shoe String Press, Inc., 1961, pp. 146-60. The most complete listing of short-story criticism to 1960.

Critical Studies

The following list emphasizes general studies rather than explications and criticisms of individual works. I have tried to minimize duplication of those items already cited in the notes, and I have been forced to make arbitrary selections out of the enormous bulk of Hemingway criticism.

BACKMAN, MELVIN. "Hemingway: The Matador and the Crucified," *Modern Fiction Studies*, I (August, 1955), 2-11. A very interesting, persuasively argued thematic attempt to locate two major forces in Hemingway's fiction.

BAKER, CARLOS, ed. *Hemingway and His Critics: An International Anthology*. New York: Hill and Wang, Inc., 1961. An interesting anthology of reprinted pieces, some translated especially for the volume. The introduction is a good survey of Hemingway's international reputation; the checklist of criticism updates Beebe's and includes many foreign listings.

BAKER, CARLOS. *Hemingway: The Writer as Artist*. Princeton: Princeton University Press, 1956. The "definitive" book on Hemingway to date, it contains more factual information than any other single source. The interpretations are always interesting, but marred by a kind of bardolatry.

BISHOP, JOHN PEALE. "The Missing All," *Virginia Quarterly Review*, XIII (Summer, 1937), 107-21. A keen appreciative essay on the effects of Hemingway's prose.

BURGUM, EDWIN BERRY. *The Novel and the World's Dilemma*. New York: Oxford University Press, 1947. An intelligent specimen of Leftist criticism which is especially useful in demonstrating Hemingway's fuzzy and contradictory use of political abstractions.

CARGILL, OSCAR. *Intellectual America: Ideas on the March*. New York: The Macmillan Company, 1948. A spirited impressionistic survey of Hemingway's work which is frequently provocative.

CARPENTER, FREDERICK I. "Hemingway Achieves the Fifth Dimension," *PMLA*, LXIX (September, 1954), 711-18. A pioneer attempt to demonstrate the relationship between Hemingway's concept of time and the aims of his aesthetic.

COLVERT, JAMES B. "Ernest Hemingway's Morality in Action," *American Literature*, XXVII (November, 1955), 372-85. An excellent analysis of Hemingway's code of morality and a defense of its guiding discipline.

COWLEY, MALCOLM. "A Portrait of Mister Papa," *Life*, XXV (Jan. 10, 1949), 86-101. A journalistic sketch in biography; useful for those facts it contains.

D'AGOSTINI, NEMI. "The Later Hemingway," *Sewanee Review*, LXVIII (Summer, 1960), 482-93. A very keen, trenchantly argued analysis of the later work.

FENTON, CHARLES A. *The Apprenticeship of Ernest Hemingway: The Early Years*. New York: Farrar, Straus and Cudahy, Inc., 1954. Indispensable for any serious study of Hemingway. At the moment this is the only reliable biography in print, as well as the best study of Hemingway's formative period.

FRIEDRICH, OTTO. "Ernest Hemingway: Joy Through Strength," *American Scholar*, XXVI (Autumn, 1957), 410, 518-30. An intelligent hostile criticism, attacking Hemingway's work on ethical and ontological grounds.

FUSSELL, EDWIN. "Hemingway and Mark Twain," *Accent*, XIV (Summer, 1954), 199-206. A thoughtful, provoking comparison of the uses of "integrity" in the two writers.

GRAHAM, JOHN. "Ernest Hemingway: The Meaning of Style," *Modern Fiction Stories*, VI (Winter, 1960-61), 298-313. In my opinion, easily the best stylistic analysis of Hemingway's work to date.

HALLIDAY, E. M. "Hemingway's Ambiguity: Symbolism and Irony," *American Literature*, XXVIII (1956), 1-22. An enormously interesting discussion of Hemingway's "realism," and a useful corrective of misreadings of Hemingway's symbolism.

—————. "Hemingway's Narrative Perspective," *Sewanee Review*, LX (Spring, 1952), 202-18. One of the best analyses of Hemingway's narrative perspective that I have found.

HART, ROBERT C. "Hemingway on Writing," *College English*, XVIII (March, 1957), 314-20. A very good short summary of Hemingway's aesthetic.

HOFFMAN, FREDERICK J. "No Beginning and No End: Hemingway and Death," *Essays in Criticism*, III (January, 1953), 73-84. A thematic study of Hemingway's attitude toward and employment of death in his fictions.

JONES, JOHN A. "Hemingway: The Critics and the Public Legend," *Western Humanities Review*, XIII (Autumn, 1959), 387-400. A most lucid, dispassionate account of the relationship of Hemingway criticism to Hemingway's work in the 1930's.

KASHKEEN, IVAN. "Ernest Hemingway: A Tragedy of Craftsmanship," *International Literature*, V (1934), 76-108. The most intelligent and sensitive example of Marxist criticism on Hemingway's work.

KILLINGER, JOHN. *Hemingway and the Dead Gods*. Lexington, Kentucky: University of Kentucky Press, 1960. An argument by analogy that Hemingway is an existentialist. It suffers from oversimple definitions and poor interpretative reading.

Selected Bibliography

LEVIN, HARRY. "Observations on the Style of Ernest Hemingway," *Kenyon Review*, XIII (Autumn, 1951), 581-609. The first serious analysis of Hemingway's style; still provocative in its illuminations.

LEWIS, WYNLHAM. "The Dumb Ox: A Study of Ernest Hemingway," *The American Review*, III (June, 1934), 289-312. The "classic" essay in vituperation, attacking both Hemingway and his work. It is egregiously unjust and magnificently alive; it remains the fountainhead of all subsequent similar attacks.

McCAFFERY, JOHN K. M., ed. *Ernest Hemingway: The Man and His Work*. Cleveland: The World Publishing Company, 1950. The first anthology of critical pieces devoted entirely to Hemingway.

MOLONEY, MICHAEL F. "Ernest Hemingway: The Missing Third Dimension." *Fifty Years of the American Novel*. Harold C. Gardiner, ed. New York: Charles Scribner's Sons 1952. An intelligent and sensitive specimen of Catholic criticism of Hemingway.

O'FAOLIAN, SEAN. *The Vanishing Hero: Studies of the Hero in the Modern Novel*. Boston: Little Brown and Company, 1956. An extremely perceptive and thorough survey of Hemingway's career and achievements.

PAOLINI, PIER FRANCESCO. "The Hemingway of the Major Works" (1956) reprinted in Baker, *Hemingway and His Critics*, pp. 131-44. A brilliant thematic study of the struggle against *nada* in Hemingway's work.

PLIMPTON, GEORGE. "Ernest Hemingway," *Paris Review*, XVIII (Spring, 1958), 61-82. An interview with Hemingway; moderately useful for its information and Hemingway's guarded remarks.

ROSENFELD, ISAAC. "A Farewell to Hemingway," *Kenyon Review*, XIII (1951), 147-55. An interesting psychoanalytic examination of Hemingway's evasion of feeling and fear of femininity.

ROSS, LILLIAN. *Portrait of Hemingway*. New York: Simon and Schuster, 1961. A reissue of *The New Yorker* "Profile" of May 13, 1950, which has been the subject of some controversy as to whether it was malicious or benevolent in portrayal.

SANDERS, DAVID. "Ernest Hemingway's Spanish Civil War Experience," *American Quarterly*, XII (Summer, 1960), 133-43. A good summary of the extent of Hemingway's political commitments in Spain.

SANDERSON, STEWART F. *Ernest Hemingway*. Edinburgh: Oliver and Boyd Ltd., 1961. An excellent, although elementary, appreciative study of Hemingway. Probably the best introduction to his work.

WARREN, ROBERT PENN. "Hemingway," *Kenyon Review*, IV (Winter, 1947), 1-28. An early, excellent analysis of Hemingway's work with special attention to the workings of the code.

WEEKS, ROBERT P., ed. *Hemingway: A Collection of Critical Essays.* Englewood Cliffs, New Jersey: Prentice-Hall, Inc., 1962. An excellent, well-diversified selection of critical pieces.

WILSON, EDMUND. "Hemingway: Bourdon Guage of Morale" (1941), reprinted in *Eight Essays.* New York: Anchor Books, 1954, pp. 92-114. A keenly perceptive exposition of the strengths and weaknesses in Hemingway's work. It is still useful.

WOOLF, VIRGINIA. "An Essay in Criticism," *New York Herald Tribune,* Oct. 9, 1927. A very keen, prophetic review of *The Sun Also Rises* and *Men Without Women* by one of the best critics of our epoch.

YOUNG, PHILIP. *Ernest Hemingway.* New York: Rinehart & Company, Inc., 1952. The most exciting interpretative study of Hemingway's work from a psychographical angle. Also, includes an interesting comparative study of Hemingway and Mark Twain. This is an indispensable book for the serious student of Hemingway.

Index

(References to Hemingway's works will be found under the author's name.)